FROM
EXODUS
TO
ADVENT

MORRIS VENDEN

FROM EXODUS TO ADVENT

Southern Publishing Association, Nashville, Tennessee

Copyright © 1980 by
Southern Publishing Association

This book was
Edited by Gerald Wheeler
Designed by Mark O'Connor

Type set: 10/12 Palatino

Printed in U.S.A.

Library of Congress Cataloging in Publication Data

Venden, Morris L
   From Exodus to Advent.

   1. Christian life—Seventh-day Adventist authors.
2. Exodus, The—Typology.   I. Title.
BV4501.2.V38   1980   248'.48'673   79-22389
ISBN 0-8127-0255-7

Contents

The Long Route Home	7
Deliverance at Midnight	18
From Egypt to Sinai	26
Melted Manna	35
Law and Gospel at Sinai	44
When God Answered Prayer Against His Will	56
We Are Still Here	66
Sleeping in the Wilderness	83
Striking the Rock, With Moses	97
You Don't Have to Know the Reason	110
So Near and Yet So Far	121
The Mighty Shaking	133
Crossing the Jordan	148
Jericho to Ai	161
The Song of Moses and the Lamb	173

Chapter 1

The Long Route Home

Have you ever wondered how long it will be until Jesus really does come again? How long can we keep saying that His return is right upon us? Why are we still here? Will God finish His mission on earth? Will He cut it short? Or is God's final conclusion to His great plan contingent upon what *we* do? Will there come a time after which God will wait no longer, regardless of what we do?

What is the purpose of church organization? How does God look at offshoots, fanatics, fringe movements? Is the God of the Old Testament as much a God of love as the God of the New Testament? Is the theme of "Salvation by Faith in Christ" only a New Testament concept?

When I was in college our Bible teacher walked into the classroom one day carrying a pile of syllabus-type books—thick, mimeographed, obviously unpublished. He told us that they would be of benefit to us, and I, along with the rest of the class, bought a copy. The author was Taylor Bunch, and it carried the title, "The Exodus and Advent Movement in Type and Antitype." At first glance it appeared exceedingly dry. My copy ended up on the bottom shelf and stayed there for years. But one day, prompted by a growing interest in the subject of salvation by faith, I took the book from the shelf, dusted it off, and began studying. I discovered it to be a most fascinating study, for we as a people are repeating the history of ancient Israel. His study answers the questions of why we are still here, what will finally bring us to the heavenly Canaan, and what is God's purpose for His church. We also find a great emphasis on the mighty love of God and on the teaching of salvation through Christ alone *in the Old Testament*.

The syllabus that I have is no longer available, but I'd like to suggest if you wish to pursue the study personally that you read the following material: the first five books of the Bible; *Patriarchs and Prophets*, the chapters that deal with the Exodus from Egypt through to the entrance into Canaan; and the book *Christ Our Righteousness*, by A. G. Daniells. Daniells, using mostly inspired material, shows how we, too, have journeyed in a spiritual wilderness.

To admit that we have aimlessly wandered, trying to learn our lessons of faith and trust, is an ego-deflating experience to our denominational pride. Perhaps as a church we have been slow to face that possibility. But let's not get bogged down in the problem of thinking about the church as being some giant, impersonal movement. The church consists of individuals. Therefore, when we discuss the church, we're talking about ourselves.

The Long Route Home

We must get rid of the idea that when we study this subject we are taking potshots at our leaders. For too long we have thought of the church as being a group of administrators. *We* are the church!

"Satan's snares are laid for us as verily as they were laid for the children of Israel just prior to their entrance into the land of Cannan. We are repeating the history of that people" (*Testimonies*, Vol. 5, p. 160). "God would have His people in these days review with a humble heart and teachable spirit the trials through which ancient Israel passed, that they may be instructed in their preparation for the heavenly Canaan" (*Patriarchs and Prophets*, p. 293).

First Corinthians 10:1-11 declares, "Moreover, brethren, I would not that ye should be ignorant, how that all our fathers were under the cloud, and all passed through the sea; and all were baptized unto Moses in the cloud and in the sea; and did all eat the same spiritual meat; and did all drink the same spiritual drink: for they drank of that spiritual Rock that followed them: and that Rock was Christ. But with many of them God was not well pleased: for they were overthrown in the wilderness. Now these things were our examples, to the intent we should not lust after evil things, as they also lusted. Neither be ye idolaters, as were some of them; as it is written, The people sat down to eat and drink, and rose up to play. Neither let us commit fornication, as some of them committed, and fell in one day three and twenty thousand. Neither let us tempt Christ, as some of them also tempted, and were destroyed of serpents. Neither murmur ye, as some of them also murmured, and were destroyed of the destroyer. Now all these things happened unto them for ensamples: and they are written for our admonition, upon whom the ends of the world are come."

Although directed to the early believers, Paul makes it quite clear that his message applies also to the end of the world. So we have lessons that we desperately need to learn from the experiences of Israel in the desert on their journey from Egypt to the Promised land.

The Bible contains a number of parallels. There are types and there are antitypes. By that we mean, for example, that Adam was a type, or figure, of Christ. We know from our study of the Scriptures that Enoch and Elijah typified those whom Christ will translate when He comes again. Moses was a type—a sample, a figure—of those Jesus will resurrect. Noah and the Flood symbolize the end of the world. The Hebrew sanctuary stood for the heavenly one. Egypt was a type of Babylon. And ancient Israel and their progress from Egypt to the Promised Land prefigured the modern Advent movement.

We need to remember that types and antitypes are not identical. They are only similar. For instance, when we talk about the lamb as a type of Christ, we do not mean that Christ has four legs and wool. Rather, a lamb represents something important about Jesus. May God help us to get the real message out of our study, to avoid the pitfalls, and to learn the lessons that we

The Long Route Home

so desperately need.

For the sake of an overview, I will try to give you the whole series of studies in the next few pages, and then in the following chapter start over with more detail.

Israel entered Egypt pure but came out a group of illiterate slaves, most of whom had given in and compromised with the Egyptian taskmasters. In the modern setting, the apostolic church slipped into ignorance and apostasy and long periods of dark ages until they came to the time of reformation, which started in the 1500s, has been going on ever since, and is not yet completed.

The Hebrews had gotten mixed up with the idolatry and the worship of the Egyptians, including bull and calf worship. Israel had become semipagan. And by the fourth generation they needed a great reformation to bring them back to the faith of their ancestors. So it has been in the antitype. The apostolic days knew a pure faith, but Paul predicted a falling away (2 Thessalonians 2). The Dark Ages almost completely extinguished spiritual light. Then reformation came. In the end we always have the forming of a separate and distinct people who have to leave Egypt or Babylon in order to worship God. God delivered ancient Israel from Egyptian bondage that they might serve Him and keep His commandments (Psalm 105:43-45). For the same purpose He has called modern Israel out of spiritual Babylon.

Just before God rescued Israel from Egypt, He poured out His judgments in ten plagues, the last seven falling on the Egyptians only. And just before He ultimately saves the Advent people from our world of persecutions and bondage, He again manifests His judgment in plagues, the final seven falling upon the wicked only. Israel's deliverance came at midnight, and the final rescue of the remnant of God comes at midnight.

God led the Exodus people, and He was visible in a pillar of fire or a cloud. But He had human leadership as well. The primary leader was Moses. Moses did not look for authority, neither did he shirk responsibility. The movement would have gone to pieces without him. But before they entered the Promised Land, after their wanderings, Moses had to die. However, he wrote the instructions necessary to take them through. Do we have a parallel to Moses in the Advent movement?

One observes some interesting things about organization in the early Exodus movement that the Advent movement, almost without realizing it, has followed. Tithes and offerings financed the Exodus. I think I even see some evidence of an Ingathering campaign, although the money gathered went into the golden calf and the people ended up drinking their ingathering. But they had gone house to house in Egypt to collect it.

The Lord rescued the Israelites from Pharaoh's armies at the Red Sea, which 1 Corinthians 10 calls their baptism. Then they traveled to a spot called Marah, a place of bitterness. The Exodus movement encountered bitter disappointment, as has the Advent movement. Shortly after their disap-

The Long Route Home

pointment they arrived at Mount Sinai and came face-to-face with the Ten Commandments. You find a parallel in the early Advent movement as well. The Sabbath was a sign and test of loyalty in both groups. Both received special instruction in healthful living and concerning the sanctuary. And both ultimately triumph and sing the song of Moses and the Lamb.

Had God chosen the shortest route to Canaan, He would not have led the Israelites to Sinai at all. But neither did He select the longest one. He guided them by way of the wilderness in order to teach them lessons of faith and trust in Him, in preparation for entering the Promised Land. After several months He directed them to Kadesh-barnea on the borders of Canaan. From there God intended to take them into Canaan. But the people got nervous. They sent spies to examine the land. They came back with their negative report, and the people began to cry and wail. "Would God we had died in this wilderness," they complained. God answered their prayer, and all of them twenty years or older, except the two men who had reported positively, died in the desert. (The movement that finally went into the Promised Land forty years later was the same movement, but a different generation.)

And so you have the people of Israel wandering around through the wilderness. At the end of thirty-eight years God evidently intended to shorten their exile, and He brought them again to Kadesh-barnea. But once more they lost heart.

They failed to follow God's instructions, evidently looking to themselves instead of to Him. As a result He had to direct them back to the desert. At this point Moses lost his patience. Do you blame him? But it's interesting to notice that whenever the children of Israel went back into the wilderness, Moses accompanied them—as did God.

Then the Israelites journeyed around Edom, a detour in which they encountered great trouble. Finally they camped on the banks of the Jordan River near a mountain called Peor. At Peor (although the people of Israel didn't know it), a man named Balaam tried to curse them, only to discover to his dismay that he could not curse what God had blessed. He went back to the king who had hired him and said, "I've got a better way. If you can in some way separate these people from their God, the curse will be automatic. You won't have to hire me to curse them." Following Balaam's suggestions, they sent cordial invitations to the people of Israel to come to a big party over at Peor. At least 24,000 went—many of them leaders. The apostasy at the Jordan River resulted in a great shake-up. God intended to take the movement across the Jordan River whether *all* the people were ready or not. A time is coming in the earth's history when God plans to take the Advent movement to the heavenly Canaan whether we all are ready or not.

The people there at the banks of the Jordan split into two groups. The rebels lost their lives. The rest of them crossed the Jordan. We have had our occasions at Kadesh-barnea in our own attempt to fit into God's mission in the last days. Many times God has obviously attempted to finish the task, and He gave us message after message designed to lead us to revival and reformation and outreach. But again and again we have tended to turn Him down, not because we weren't interested, but because we wanted to do it our way. *Our* way, instead of His.

In their study of the Exodus and Advent comparison, some of our historians have argued on one extreme: "We have failed God and have wandered in the wilderness and will continue to do so." On the other hand, we have historians who announce optimistically, "God's power and the outpouring of the Holy Spirit and the latter rain began in the last century and have been going on ever since."

I remember going to a General Conference in Cleveland some years ago. Having just studied this subject, I was quite interested in finding all of the old pioneers at the General Conference and began to ask around as to who and where they were. Someone said, "You should go to see such and such a man. He helped begin the church in the Southern states." I found him in his hotel, and in the lobby we sat and talked—that is, we shouted. In his nineties, he was almost deaf and blind. Although hardly able to move, his mind was still clear. He shouted to me there in the hotel lobby, "Brother, we have been wandering in the wilderness." But the historians don't all agree with that.

The greatest proof that we *have* failed is the fact that we are still here. You can't argue with that. Also we read statements, like the one found in

Selected Messages, Book One, p. 234: "An unwillingness to yield up preconceived opinions, and to accept this truth, lay at the foundation of a large share of the opposition manifested at Minneapolis against the Lord's message through Brethren [E. J.] Waggoner and [A. T.] Jones. By exciting that opposition Satan succeeded in shutting away from our people, in a great measure, the special power of the Holy Spirit that God longed to impart to them. . . . The light that is to lighten the whole earth with its glory was resisted, and by the action of our own brethren has been *in a great degree* kept away from the world."

A statement like that is always conspicuously absent from the records of the optimistic historians. You can't argue with it. And you can't debate the fact that we are still here and that people are still dying. But I'd like to propose that a group of people called the remnant will yet demonstrate that our primary mission to the world is to teach what true salvation through faith in Christ alone is all about.

"It was not the will of God that Israel should wander forty years in the wilderness. . . . In like manner, it was not the will of God that the coming of Christ should be so long delayed and His people should remain so many years in this world of sin and sorrow" (*The Great Controversy*, p. 458).

Here again you have both movements put into the same package. It was because they failed to learn the lessons of faith and trust that the Exodus people wandered so long in the wilderness. (And we are repeating their history.) But all the way you see God with them. His pillar of fire and His cloud accompanied them. God has stayed with His remnant people, too. He has kept on loving us. It ought to give us a mighty incentive to keep on loving Him in return. And we should thank Him not only for His mercy and patience with the Exodus people but for His long-suffering with His Advent people as well.

Chapter 2

Deliverance at Midnight

Thutmose I was king of Egypt, but he didn't have an heir to his throne. The closest he had to one was his daughter, Hatshepsut. However, Egypt had never had a woman king. One day, when she and her maidens walked along the Nile River, they discovered a baby in the bulrushes, and Hatshepsut got a bright idea. She could adopt a son. The son she could train to become heir to the throne of Egypt.

You know the rest of the story. At age twelve the babe rescued from the bulrushes began his training in the military academy in preparation for his glorious task of becoming king of Egypt. But his real mother had taught him eternal values during his childhood, and he chose rather to suffer affliction with the people of God than to enjoy the pleasures of being king for a time. After Moses disappeared from the scene, Hatshepsut became the "king" of Egypt for a short period. Then she became frightened because some of the rest of the Egyptian leaders weren't too excited about her being ruler. She united with her boyfriend, Senmut, to defend herself against treachery. Apparently her fears were well-grounded, for Hatshepsut and Senmut soon disappeared from the record of Egyptian history. Thutmose III became the new king, reigning on the throne that Moses could have occupied.

God had told Moses that He wanted him to lead Israel out of Egypt. Moses thought God had picked the right man, and instead of waiting for Him to direct operations, he began to do the job in his own way. He got one Egyptian. Then he had to flee into the wilderness, where for forty years the Lord used sheep to teach Moses the lesson of dependence on Him. Finally Moses learned that God does not need man to fight His battles for Him. At last he was willing to allow God to deliver His people in His own way. And God appeared in a fiery bush and directed him to return to Egypt.

Aaron, Moses' brother and spokesman, met him in the wilderness, and they traveled to Egypt together. The first thing they did when they arrived was to call the people of Israel together to tell them the good news that the time had come for God to free them from slavery. "And the people believed: and when they heard that the Lord had visited the children of Israel, and that he had looked upon their affliction, then they bowed their heads and worshipped" (Exodus 4:31).

Moses and Aaron must have felt encouraged. Things were falling into place. Back at the burning bush, one of Moses' first concerns had been whether or not the people of Israel would believe that God had sent him (Exodus 3:13). But they did, and Moses and Aaron went to break the news to the king.

Pharaoh didn't like the idea. "Who is the Lord, that I should obey his voice to let Israel go? I know not the Lord, neither will I let Israel go" (Exodus 5:2). Instead of releasing them, he increased their loads and their labors. The Hebrews discovered that all of a sudden they didn't believe so well anymore. Even Moses apparently doubted whether or not God knew what He was doing, for we hear him praying, "Since I came to Pharaoh to speak in thy name, he hath done evil to this people: neither hast thou delivered thy people *at all**" (verse 23).

So God began His softening-up process with the first of the ten plagues. After the flies infested Egypt, Pharaoh summoned Moses and Aaron and said, "Go ye, sacrifice to your God *in the land*" (Exodus 8:25).

Moses replied, "It is not meet so to do; for we shall sacrifice the abomination of the Egyptians to the Lord our God" (verse 26).

And then, when they insisted, Pharaoh said, "*Don't go very far*" Exodus 8:25-28).

The plagues continued. After the hail Pharaoh summoned Moses and Aaron again. They had a message for him that if he did not free the Hebrews, the Lord would send locusts to clean up whatever the hail had missed. By then Pharaoh's own ser-

---

*Emphasis in Bible texts supplied by author unless otherwise noted.

Deliverance At Midnight

vants had begun encouraging him to give in. So Pharaoh grudgingly told Moses, "Go, serve the Lord your God: but who are they that shall go?

"And Moses said, We will go with our young and with our old, with our sons and with our daughters, with our flocks and with our herds will we go; for we must hold a feast unto the Lord" (Exodus 10:8, 9).

"Not so," the Egyptian ruler retorted. "*Just the men may go.*" That's a little different than today. Now it's usually the women and children that become the church members. It's sort of refreshing to see that the appeal back there was to the men.

So the locusts came, and after that the darkness. "And Pharaoh called unto Moses and said, Go ye, serve the Lord; only *let your flocks and your herds be stayed:* let your little ones also go with you" (verse 24). What happens when people leave their possessions in Egypt? Many of us have gone through something similar. But Moses and Aaron persisted, and finally the angel slew the firstborn. Then Pharaoh "called for Moses and Aaron by night, and said, Rise up, and get you forth from among my people, both ye and the children of Israel; and go, serve the Lord, as ye have said. Also take your flocks and your herds, as ye have said, and be gone; and *bless me also*" (Exodus 12:31, 32).

Pharaoh went through the following sequence: (1) Sacrifice within the land. (2) Don't go far. (3) Go, but leave part of the family. (4) Go, but leave your possessions. (5) Just go. All of you. Take everything you have. And bless me also. (6)

Then he runs after them.

That phrase, "Bless me also," has always intrigued me. One day everyone who has ever lived or died meets together for the first and last time. Some of them stand inside of a giant city, looking out. The rest wait on the outside, looking in. Finally, somewhere upon a rise above the throngs encircling the city, their leader drops to his knees and acknowledges that God has been fair and just and righteous in everything He has done. You can almost hear him saying, "Bless me also." But then the spirit that has controlled his life for centuries wells up again, and he rushes out like a madman among the masses outside the city gates. He tries to whip them up to a frenzy, telling them that they can take the city.

But back to that last midnight in Egypt. Have you ever wondered what you were celebrating at the Communion Service? Often we go back simply to the upper room in Jerusalem, with the disciples at the table with Jesus. But that wasn't the beginning. They were celebrating the Passover. Exodus 12 states, . . . "And the Lord spake unto Moses and Aaron in the land of Egypt, saying, Speak ye unto all the congregation of Israel, saying, In the tenth day of this month they shall take to them every man a lamb, according to the house of their fathers, a lamb for an house. . . . And ye shall keep it up until the fourteenth day of the same month: and the whole assembly of the congregation of Israel shall kill it in the evening.

"And they shall take of the blood, and strike it

Deliverance At Midnight 23

on the two side posts and on the upper door post of the houses, wherein they shall eat it. . . . And thus shall ye eat it; with your loins girded, your shoes on your feet, and your staff in your hand; and ye shall eat it in haste: it is the Lord's passover. For I will pass through the land of Egypt this night, and will smite all the firstborn in the land of Egypt, both man and beast; and against all the gods of Egypt I will execute judgment: I am the Lord. And the blood shall be to you for a token upon the houses where ye are: and when I see the blood, I will pass over you, and the plague shall not be upon you to destroy you, when I smite the land of Egypt. And this day shall be unto you for a memorial; and ye shall keep it a feast to the Lord throughout your generations" (Exodus 12:1-14).

All the plagues have fallen except that last one. If you are the firstborn, you don't feel like sleeping. You've heard the instruction. It's gone throughout Israel's settlements. Now you toss and turn in bed, with your shoes, jeans, and sweat shirt on. You're going to leave shortly after midnight. As you toss and turn, you call, "Father."

"Yes, Son."

"Have you killed the lamb?"

"Not yet, Son. We've got plenty of time. It's only 10:00 PM."

Or can you imagine something like this: "Father, have you done what the Lord said?"

"Yes, I've killed the lamb."

"Did you sprinkle the blood?"

"No, we didn't do that."

"Father!"

How would you feel if you were the firstborn? Suppose you said, "Father have you killed the lamb and sprinkled the blood?"

"Yes."

"Did you sprinkle the blood on the two side posts and on the upper doorpost?"

"Oh, Son, that's legalistic. We believe in righteousness by faith. God loves everybody. He wouldn't hurt anyone."

Righteousness by faith does not cause us to lower our attention to God's instruction one whit. It never has, and it never will. Here is where some of the misunderstandings about righteousness by faith come in. A cheap version floating around makes people say, "God won't hurt anybody. Don't get all shook up about this or that detail."

Some people have the idea that God is not particular. But we don't find it in this story—nor in the entire Bible. And if you had been one of the firstborn that night, you'd have been particular. If you had a father who loved you, who believed that God meant what He said, he would have put the blood on the two sides of the doorpost and the upper doorpost, and he'd have done it *early*. He wouldn't have waited until 11:45.

In the godly home where the father believed, we would have seen a firstborn son who was almost able to sleep because he had a father and mother who obeyed what God says. They loved and trusted Him. And when in Egypt the wailing and the screaming sounded, in the homes with the

Deliverance At Midnight

blood on the doorposts there was great rejoicing.

The time when God delivers His people at midnight will come again. "It is at midnight that God manifests His power for the deliverance of His people" (*The Great Controversy*, p. 636). "Jesus rides forth as a mighty conqueror. . . . With anthems of celestial melody and the holy angels, a vast, unnumbered throng, attend Him on His way. The firmament seems filled with radiant forms" (*ibid.*, p. 641). Probably some of those same angels who passed over Egypt that night will be in the throng of angels who join in the "anthems of celestial melody."

Our deliverance in that day will come as a result of our continued acceptance of the covering of the blood of the Lamb. "And when I see the blood, I will pass over you." "As the nations of the saved look upon their Redeemer and behold the eternal glory of the Father shining in His countenance; as they behold His throne, which is from everlasting to everlasting, and know that His kingdom is to have no end, they break forth in rapturous song: 'Worthy, worthy is the Lamb that was slain, and hath redeemed us to God by His own most precious blood!' " (*ibid.*, pp. 651, 652).

Chapter 3

From Egypt to Sinai

Evangelists have sometimes advertised their meetings with full-color posters depicting the world going up in smoke. They have spent the opening night on the subject of doomsday, showing how everything is going to pieces. But I remember what a peace came to my own heart when I saw some evangelists advertising their first meeting with, "Millions Brokenhearted, Longing for Heaven." And the people came out to hear what they had to say. So it was with the children of Israel. God's first appeal to them involved the promise of a land flowing with milk and honey. Even though they did not realize their low spiritual condition, the Promised Land looked good to them. God's second appeal was to try to show them their need of a trust relationship with Him. He did not lay on them the burden of getting themselves to the Promised Land but tried patiently to teach them to depend upon Him. And His third appeal had to do with the Ten Commandments and His standard of obedience. How often we have gotten God's order just backwards.

From Egypt to Sinai

God's people left Egypt at midnight, unhindered, just as He had promised. They began their journey, following the pillars of fire and cloud, toward the Red Sea. Hardly had they had time to wonder how they would get to the other side of the Red Sea or past the mountains that were on either side when the report circulated that Pharaoh and his armies approached from behind. It looked like a trap. And the people began the routine that they followed unvaryingly for the next forty years. First they grouched and grumbled because things weren't going just right. Next they blamed Moses for all their trouble. Then they began to think that Egypt hadn't been so bad after all. And finally they concluded that they were now going to die in the wilderness.

Exodus 14:10-14 tells us about their impasse at the Red Sea: "And when Pharaoh drew nigh, the children of Israel lifted up their eyes, and, behold, the Egyptians marched after them; and they were sore afraid: and the children of Israel cried out unto the Lord. And they said unto Moses, Because there were no graves in Egypt, hast thou taken us away to die in the wilderness? wherefore hast thou dealt thus with us, to carry us forth out of Egypt? Is this not the word that we did tell thee in Egypt, saying, Let us alone, that we may serve the Egyptians? For it had been better for us to serve the Egyptians, than that we should die in the wilderness. And Moses said unto the people, Fear ye not, stand still, and see the salvation of the Lord, which he will shew to you to day: for the Egyptians whom ye have seen to day, ye shall see them again no more for ever. The Lord shall fight for you, and ye shall hold your peace."

Sometimes we say, "Don't just stand there. Do something!" Moses said "Don't just do something. Stand there." That's what he told them: "Stand still. The Lord is going to fight for you." In verse 15, "The Lord said unto Moses, Wherefore criest thou unto me? speak unto the children of Israel that they go forward." Notice that the issue here is that they were to stand still in relation to fighting the enemy. But they were to go forward in relationship to God's guidance in the path He had for them.

The Lord had never commanded them that they should fight for the Promised Land. "It was not His purpose that they should gain the land by warfare, but by strict obedience to His commands" (*Patriarchs and Prophets*, p. 392). God can use the simplest methods, such as those listed in Exodus 23:27, 28: "I will send my fear before thee, and will destroy all the people to whom thou shalt come, and I will make all thine enemies turn their backs unto thee. And I will send hornets before thee, which shall drive out the Hivite, the Canaanite, and the Hittite, from before thee." The only way you would think it a ridiculous method would be if you had never been stung by one. God had His own arsenal, but the people had a hard time believing it.

So here they are at the Red Sea. Some people say God told them to go down to the water, and when their feet touched it the water parted. But they are

From Egypt to Sinai

thinking of the Hebrews' experience at the end of their wilderness wanderings, at the Jordan River. Could it be that they were a little better able to trust God then than they were at the beginning? But it still must have taken a degree of faith to march through the Red Sea.

The famous faith chapter makes only two references to the Exodus movement. Hebrews 11:29 states, "By faith they passed through the Red sea as by dry land: which the Egyptians assaying to do were drowned." And the other instance occurs at the end of their wilderness wanderings. "By faith the walls of Jericho fell down" (verse 30). So it took faith to go through the Red Sea.

The next morning, when the people were on the other side, they looked back. Evidently there had been a terrible storm—earthquake and lightning and thunder and torrents of rain from heaven, as well as the sea crashing together. As the people looked back they saw the bodies of their enemies who had washed ashore.

"The history of ancient Israel is a striking illustration of the past experience of the Adventist body. God led His people in the advent movement, even as He led the children of Israel from Egypt. In the great disappointment their faith was tested as was that of the Hebrews at the Red Sea. Had they still trusted to the guiding hand that had been with them in their past experience, they would have seen of the salvation of God. If all who had labored unitedly in the work in 1844, had received the third angel's message and proclaimed it in the power of the Holy Spirit, the Lord would have wrought mightily with their efforts. A flood of light would have been shed upon the world. *Years ago* the inhabitants of the earth would have been warned, the closing work completed, and Christ would have come for the redemption of His people" (*The Great Controversy*, pp. 457, 458, emphasis supplied). Ellen White wrote *that* in the 1880s. "Years ago" Christ might have come.

No wonder some preachers and writers have taken up the question, asking "How near is near?" You can say for a hundred years that it's right around the corner, but what do you mean by that? We'll find its answer as we proceed.

Some people have gotten the idea that maybe the 1844 movement was a rather naive, childish thing the people went through. They have the feeling that people got involved in a big mistake. I've heard some Adventist intellectuals say that the 1844 movement represented us in our childhood, and since then we've grown up. We're more intellectual and sophisticated now.

Notice a description of what happened in 1844 by one who was there: "Of all the great religious movements since the days of the apostles, none have been more free from human imperfection and the wiles of Satan than was that of the autumn of 1844. Even now, after the lapse of many years, all who shared in that movement and who have stood firm upon the platform of truth still feel the holy influence of that blessed work and bear witness that it was of God" (*ibid.*, p. 401).

From Egypt to Sinai

"The advent movement of 1840-1844 was a glorious manifestation of the power of God; the first angel's message was carried to every missionary station in the world, and in some countries there was the greatest religious interest which has been witnessed in any land since the Reformation of the sixteenth century; but these are to be exceeded by the mighty movement under the last warning of the third angel" (*ibid.*, p. 611).

So let's not say that it was some childish, naive thing that happened back there. It was a great manifestation of God's power. And who were the Advent people in 1844? Baptists, Methodists, Presbyterians, Congregationalists, and you name it. Our study isn't limited to Seventh-day Adventists.

As the Exodus people followed the cloud from the Red Sea, the first place they came to had the name of Marah. By that time they were thirsty. But Moses knew the country. As the people caught sight of the oasis and rushed forward to the water, his heart sank within him. He knew what kind of water was there. And then he heard their cries and complaints. People who had been singing and dancing a little while before began to gripe again. "Did you bring us out here to die of thirst?"

"God leads His people on, step by step. He brings them up to different points calculated to manifest what is in the heart. Some endure at one point, but fall off at the next. At every advanced point the heart is tested and tried a little closer" (*Testimonies*, Vol. 1, p. 187). So God exposes His people to experiences designed to try them and show them what faith is all about. If they fail one test, He leads them over the same ground again and again, with increased pressure, until they finally learn the lesson He wants to teach them.

God sweetened Marah's bitter waters, and from there they traveled through the desert to a place called Elim. Elim had seventy palm trees and twelve wells of water. It is a beautiful place. The people must have been wonderfully refreshed after spending some time there.

Then the cloud moved forward once more, into the Wilderness of Sin. There they ran out of food, and God gave them manna to eat. Remember that this began approximately six weeks before God gave the Ten Commandments at Mount Sinai, and it has always been a rebuke to the person who wants to say that Sabbath observance started at Mount Sinai through the Ten Commandment law of the Jews, as they call it. From Marah through the wilderness, God demonstrated that He still had a special regard for one seventh of their time, the Sabbath.

As they continued to travel through the Wilderness of Sin they came to a place named Rephidim. Again thirsty and with no water, they once more began complaining, deciding that probably the best thing to do would be to stone Moses, who had brought them on this pointless trip. God told Moses to strike the rock, and water came gushing out. The rock represented Jesus, and the water symbolized Jesus and the Holy Spirit.

What significance does the incident have for the

Advent people today? In *Selected Messages*, Book One, p. 343, we read, "All that man can possibly do toward his own salvation is to accept the invitation, 'Whosoever will, let him take the water of life freely' (Revelation 22:17)." But what is the water of life? The same author describes it on page 113 of *Thoughts From the Mount of Blessing:* "In this communion with Christ, through prayer and the study of the great and precious truths of His word, we shall as hungry souls be fed; as those that thirst, we shall be refreshed at the fountain of life." To take the water of life freely is to have fellowship and communion with Christ through prayer and the study of His Word. And that is all that I can do toward my own salvation.

God provided bread from heaven and water from the rock for the Exodus people. He knew they would perish in the Wilderness of Sin without these. But the only ones who received benefit from His provisions were those who ate of the bread and drank of the water. Eating and drinking are individual matters. All that the Israelites could possibly do was to partake of the nourishment God provided. To refuse was to die.

"Oh, I'm trying hard to be a good person, to live a good moral life. I wouldn't think of doing anything bad." No, that's not the issue. How much time do you spend drinking the water of life? Without it you will die spiritually, just as surely as you will perish physically without food or drink.

In spite of the fact that God told the Exodus people they would not need to fight, we see them at

Rephidim scrapping with the Amalekites. What happened to the hornets? Did God want them to fight for themselves? Wasn't He going to battle *for* them? Or was it their lack of faith that led them to wage their own skirmish?

Even before you had faith, God was guiding your life. As I've looked back over my own life I've been amazed at the instances of God's leading when I didn't yet know what it was to walk with Him. Even before the Hebrews, having come out of slavery, understood much about God, God directed their lives. In spite of their murmurings and complainings, He stayed with them through all the rocky defiles and gravelly passes of the desert. In your own experience you may have walked a similar route. It looked like a dead-end street right ahead of you—sorrow or trouble or pain or sickness or disappointment. You felt you were all alone out there in the wilderness. But, then, as you glance back, you realize that God was guiding you. And He still is. The God who led Israel from Egypt to Canaan is still in charge. He has lessons of faith and trust to teach us today so that He can take us through to the Promised Land tomorrow.

Chapter 4

Melted Manna

The people of Israel had been out of Egypt for about six weeks. Now, on the way to Sinai, just past Elim with its palm trees and wells of water, they got hungry. "Too bad we didn't die before we left Egypt," they grumbled. "At least we would have died with full stomachs. Now we're hungry, and it's all Moses' fault!"

"And the Lord spake unto Moses, saying, I have heard the murmurings of the children of Israel: speak unto them, saying, At even ye shall eat flesh, and in the morning ye shall be filled with bread; and ye shall know that I am the Lord your God.

"And it came to pass, that at even the quails came up, and covered the camp: and in the morning the dew lay round about the host. And when the dew that lay was gone up, behold, upon the face of the wilderness there lay a small round thing, as small as the hoar frost on the ground. And when the children of Israel saw it, they said one to another, It is manna: for they wist not what it was" (Exodus 16:11-15). (*Manna* means, "What is it?" So what they said was, "It is what is it!") They recognized the quail, but they didn't know what angels' food was.)

"And Moses said unto them, This is the bread which the Lord hath given you to eat. This is the thing which the Lord hath commanded, Gather of it every man according to his eating, an omer for every man, according to the number of your persons; take ye every man for them which are in his tents. And the children of Israel did so, and gathered, some more, some less. And when they did mete it with an omer, he that gathered much had nothing over, and he that gathered little had no lack; they gathered every man according to his eating. And Moses said, Let no man leave of it till the morning. Notwithstanding they hearkened not unto Moses; but some of them left of it until the morning, and it bred worms and stank: and Moses was wroth with them. And they gathered it every morning, every man according to his eating: and when the sun waxed hot, it melted" (verses 15-21).

Jesus used the manna to represent a great spiritual truth. "I am that bread of life. Your fathers did eat manna in the wilderness, and are dead. This is the bread which cometh down from heaven, that a man may eat thereof, and not die. I am the living bread which came down from heaven: if any man eat of this bread, he shall live for ever: and the bread that I will give is my flesh, which I will give for the life of the world. The Jews therefore strove among themselves, saying, How can this man give us his flesh to eat?" (John 6:48-52).

Cannibals would have easily misunderstood

Melted Manna

His words. The Jewish leaders, who should have known better, argued over them, and even the disciples were confused. But Jesus explained, "The words that I speak unto you, they are spirit and they are life" (John 6:63).

The evidence is that the Jewish leaders understood more than they wanted to. But manna, the bread from heaven, is still available today. A remarkable commentary on this Scripture appeared in *The Review and Herald* for November 23, 1897. "The reception of the Word, the bread from heaven, is declared to be the reception of Christ himself. As the Word of God is received into the soul, we partake of the flesh and blood of the Son of God. . . . Man is called upon to eat and masticate the Word; but unless his heart is open to the entrance of that Word, unless he drinks in the Word, unless he is taught of God, there will be a misconception, misapplication, and misinterpretation of that Word.

"As the blood is formed in the body by the food eaten, so Christ is formed within by eating of the Word of God, which is his flesh and blood. [So the manna, the flesh and blood, are God's Word.] He who feeds upon that Word has Christ formed within, the hope of glory. The written Word introduces to the searcher the flesh and blood of the Son of God. . . . As the necessity for temporal food cannot be supplied by once partaking of it, so the Word of God must be daily eaten to supply the spiritual necessities. . . .

"By reason of the waste and loss, the body must

be renewed with blood, by being supplied with daily food. So there is need of constantly feeding upon the Word, the knowledge of which is eternal life. That Word must be our meat and drink. It is in this alone that the soul will find its nourishment and vitality."

If you have ever tried to figure out what's tangible about living the Christian life, you've discovered three things: God's Word, prayer, and service for others. How much time do you spend with God's Word and in prayer? The tragic thing is that so many professed Christians are doing everything else but that.

It gets so tricky because we can go on living day after day with apparently healthy bodies and minds. We can work and play and take care of the temporal duties as if we were alive, when spiritually we are dead. And this condition is the result of our having starved to death spiritually.

When babies come along to bless a home the parents have the responsibility of feeding them and eventually of teaching them to feed themselves. I made a deal with my wife that if she'd have them, I'd get up with them. Now I don't know what made me make such a bargain, because she wanted them anyway. It was the worst deal I ever made. Everybody else's babies started sleeping through the night after the first few weeks. Not ours! Nine months, ten months, and I was still having to get up with them. After a while you learn how to walk in your sleep.

But suppose we decided that we wanted our

babies to start walking when they were nine months old, just like those down the street, instead of waiting until they were a year and a half (which is humiliating, you know). So we concluded that the best way to help things along was to keep the babies from getting too fat so their little legs wouldn't have such a heavy load to carry. Thus we fed them only once a week (and then, instead of giving them milk, we gave them gluten burgers). Soon we wouldn't have to worry about their walking at nine months, or at all.

Ridiculous? But in our spiritual life, we often try the same thing. Hopefully on Sabbath we receive the sincere milk of the Word. (We may even go deeper into the heavier food.) But then how many of us starve ourselves for the rest of the week?

A preacher has something far more important to do than to feed the people on Sabbath—he should teach them how to feed themselves!

It seems to me that the analogy of John 6 contains one of the greatest lessons for the people of God wandering in the wilderness today. Let's start with the first clue from the passage in Exodus 16:16: "This is the thing which the Lord hath commanded, Gather of it every man according to his eating." Suppose that I hear about some great theologian who studies his Bible and prays for four hours a day, and I say, "I guess I'd better do that too." I try it, and it doesn't work for me. Long before the four hours are up, I fall asleep.

Charles Atlas, it is said, could do two hundred pushups. I collapse after doing ten. Maybe someday I will also be able to do two hundred. But not if I just sit around waiting for it to happen. I have to keep doing my ten in the meantime. "Gather of it every man *according to his eating*." But at least gather and eat.

The context of verses 16 to 18 is that the heads of families went out to gather enough manna for their families. They were to collect no more than they could eat. Perhaps there's a lesson here. Have you ever been in a situation where the head of the family assembles everyone for family worship. It is late, the children are sleepy, and the father reads for forty-five minutes. Or perhaps he dosen't read that long but prays clear around the world, and some of them fall asleep on their knees. Perhaps the father wonders why nobody has any interest in family worship—when he has been choking them to death. "Gather of it every man according to his eating."

But although the heads of the family could collect the manna, when it came to eating it, everyone had to do it for himself. The baby has to be fed, yes. But he's the one who has to chew it, or gum it, or whatever he does with his Gerber's baby food. He's the one who has to assimilate it. It's impossible for one person to have spiritual life for another. Eating is a private, personal affair.

"And Moses said, Let no man leave of it till the morning" (verse 19). Yesterday's experience is no good for today. Today's will not serve for tomorrow. Last summer's experience is not adequate for now.

Melted Manna

During the summer between my junior and senior years in college I went to Nebraska to work as a colporteur. My mother put *The Colporteur Evangelist* into my suitcase. I couldn't have cared less about reading that book, until I found myself in the Sand Hills. Twenty-five thousand acres for each ranch. It took thirty acres to feed one cow. Out there, going from windmill to windmill, farmhouse to farmhouse, suddenly that book was my most valued possession. You soon discover that you cannot sell the books—that only God can. Circumstances drive you to your knees, to a fellowship with God that you never had at any other time.

But when I went back to school for my next year, I neglected God's Word and prayer. Riding high on the previous summer's spiritual experience, I felt that I didn't need communion with God now that I wasn't out there in the Sand Hills trying to sell books. Consequently I ended up worse off than ever. Depending on yesterday's experience for today doesn't work. "Notwithstanding they hearkened not unto Moses; but some of them left of it until the morning, and it bred worms, and stank. . . .

"And they gathered it every morning, every man according to his eating: and when the sun waxed hot, it melted." Here's another clue. Manna melts. God sent it to give the people daily strength. When do we need strength for the day? At the beginning? Or after it is over? One of the secrets of a meaningful, consistent fellowship with God is to schedule it at some earlier time than those last few minutes just before you fall asleep at night, when you can't keep your mind on the subject and you go to sleep praying.

Fellowship with God involves more than making a list and checking it twice to make sure that we have confessed all our sins. Communion with Him demands time spent in coming to know Him, not just spasmodically, but as regularly as we partake of physical nourishment. Not just a text for the day with your hand on the doorknob, but at least as much time as you spend in eating for physical growth. Meet God in the morning, when the manna is heavy on the ground. "When the sun waxed hot, it melted."

"And it came to pass, that on the sixth day they gathered twice as much." Maybe the analogy breaks down, but someone suggested to me that there might even be something there. In a typical church home, by the time Friday is over and the shoes are polished and the showers taken and the lawn mowed and house cleaned and the Sabbath meals prepared, everything is ready for Sabbath. Only everybody is also mad at everybody else. Maybe we need a double portion on Friday morning just to get through the day! But on Sabbath, the manna lies six feet deep all through the day as Jesus comes near for communion with His people.

"Oh," someone says, "I don't need that. I'm getting along fine without that manna." But wait a minute. Not only are you starving to death, whether you realize it or not, but there's Someone else involved. Someone interested in having fellowship with you. Revelation says He stands at the door and knocks. Here's something far more important than whether you happen to feel hungry or sense your need at the moment. The Creator of the universe knocks at your door. You don't think you need Him? But He needs you! You don't want Him? But He wants you!

"Behold, I stand at the door, and knock. If any man hear my voice, and open the door, I will come in" (Revelation 3:20). And He brings food with Him. Manna. Food from heaven. Angels' food. May we accept it today, tomorrow, the next day, and every day until Jesus comes again.

Chapter 5

Law and Gospel at Sinai

"In the third month, when the children of Israel were gone forth out of the land of Egypt, the same day came they into the wilderness of Sinai. For they were departed from Rephidim, and were come to the desert of Sinai, and had pitched in the wilderness; and there Israel camped before the mount. And Moses went up unto God, and the Lord called unto him out of the mountain, saying, Thus shalt thou say to the house of Jacob, and tell the children of Israel; Ye have seen what I did unto the Egyptians, and how I bare you on eagles' wings, and brought you unto myself.

"Now therefore, if ye will obey my voice indeed, and keep my covenant, then ye shall be a peculiar treasure unto me above all people: for all the earth is mine: and ye shall be unto me a kingdom of priests, and an holy nation. These are the words which thou shalt speak unto the children of Israel. And Moses came and called for the elders of the people, and laid before their faces all these words which the Lord commanded him. And all the people answered together, and said, All that the

Law and Gospel at Sinai

Lord hath spoken we will do" (Exodus 19:1-8).

This is not the only time such a statement shows up in the history of the Exodus people. Again and again in self-confidence they said, "All that the Lord hath spoken *we will do.*" Those who have debated the covenants have tried to decide if it was the proper response for them to make. Some claim that you couldn't ask for a better one. If the Lord should come down to the nearest mountain today and give you a message, "From now on I don't want you to sin anymore," what would you reply?

"All right, I promise. I'll never make any more mistakes. I vow never to sin again."

Would that be a good answer?

Suppose God came down and not only announced His Ten Commandments but also added specific instructions about how to treat servants and slaves and widows and orphans and strangers and the poor—things that we hadn't been doing. And suppose He spent as much time spelling out exactly what He meant as He did in the rest of Exodus and Leviticus and Deuteronomy.

God revealed a great number of things to His people at Sinai. He disclosed to them principles of healthful living and of organization. It's interesting that He had them ultimately grouped somewhat like the military today. The Lord told them something about finance—that one tenth of their possessions belonged to God. They learned about time—that one seventh of it was God's in a special sense. God taught them about honesty, about vows and true and false witnessing. The Hebrews learned about dress standards and marriage and divorce principles.

If the Lord were to come personally today and give us that much detailed instruction, would we say, "All right, we accept it. All You have said we will do"? It seems it would be far better to say something like Isaiah did when he stood in the presence of God: "Woe is me! for I am undone; because I am a man of unclean lips, and I dwell in the midst of a people of unclean lips: for mine eyes have seen the King, the Lord of hosts" (Isaiah 6:5).

All that the Lord has said we will do? That's too big an order! Looking at ourselves, there's not a chance in the world we can fulfill that. The only possible way we could do that would be if somehow God would write His law into our very being. We're in trouble and need help. We must have a power that we don't have.

The book *Patriarchs and Prophets,* pp. 371, 372, clearly presents the issue. "God brought them to Sinai; He manifested His glory; He gave them His law, with the promise of great blessings on condition of obedience. . . . the people did not realize the sinfulness of their own hearts, and that without Christ it was impossible for them to keep God's law; and they readily entered into covenant with God. Feeling that they were able to establish their own righteousness, they declared, 'All that the Lord hath said will we do, and be obedient.' Exodus 24:7. They had witnessed the proclamation of the law in awful majesty, and had trembled with terror before the mount; and yet only a few weeks passed before . . ." What happened? All that the Lord had said, they *didn't* do. " . . . they broke their covenant with God, and bowed down to worship a graven image.

"They could not hope for the favor of God through a covenant which they had broken; and now, seeing their sinfulness and their need of pardon, they were brought to feel their need of the Saviour revealed in the Abrahamic covenant and shadowed forth in the sacrificial offerings. Now by faith and love they were bound to God as their deliverer from the bondage of sin. Now they were prepared to appreciate the blessings of the new covenant."

Theologians have debated the issue. Did God give them an Old Covenant that they could not keep to play games with them? Would a good and kind God do that?

I'm not sure we need to answer the question. The one thing we can nail down is that when we say, "All that the Lord hath said *we* will do," we're in trouble and have fallen into a wrong relationship to the covenants.

After the Lord spoke the Ten Commandments from Mount Sinai, Moses went up into the mountain. It was dark, with thunder, lightning, earthquakes, blackness. He was gone for almost six weeks. The mixed multitude, who tried to travel to Canaan while their hearts remained in Egypt, started the campaign to return to Egypt. Rebellion spread throughout the camp. With some help from Moses' weak brother, Aaron, the people soon danced around a golden calf.

Aaron had gone along with the idea, telling himself, "The people don't really have to worship this golden calf. It can just represent the true God who delivered them." Nebuchadnezzar reasoned the same way. "You three Hebrew worthies—you don't have to worship my *image*. Kneel down and say a prayer to your own God. That'll be enough. Just don't spoil the party." So it has always gone. Luther spoke out against the same excuse. People who bow down to images use the same rationalization today. "We're not worshiping the images themselves. We use them only to help us visualize the true God."

While the people danced around the calf, Moses returned. He broke the tables of stone that God had cut out. Wresting the golden calf from its position, he ground it to powder, poured it into the water, and made the people drink their god. Then he stood in the middle of the congregation and asked for all of those who were on the Lord's side to assemble at his right. All of the tribe of Levi came, and others from every tribe. But some, in spite of everything, could still remain there and say, "We rebel." Moses told the people who had repented to take their swords, and they killed three thousand brothers, neighbors, and companions.

I might ask myself, "Where is the mercy? Why couldn't they have just let the three thousand return to Egypt? They wanted to go back. Why not have given them their choice?" Immediately I begin to find out about my attitude toward God. If I

Law and Gospel at Sinai

am already suspicious of Him, then the bloody story gives me a place to hang my doubts. But if I have already learned to love and trust God and know that He is all wise, then I keep on trusting Him in spite of the episode.

"So with the apostasy at Sinai. Unless punishment had been speedily visited upon transgression, the same results would again have been seen. The earth would have become as corrupt as in the days of Noah. Had these transgressors been spared, evils would have followed, greater than resulted from sparing the life of Cain. It was the mercy of God that thousands should suffer, to prevent the necessity of visiting judgments upon millions. In order to save the many, He must punish the few. Furthermore, as the people had cast off their allegiance to God, they had forfeited the divine protection, and, deprived of their defense, the whole nation was exposed to the power of their enemies. Had not the evil been promptly put away, they would soon have fallen a prey to their numerous and powerful foes.

"It was necessary for the good of Israel, and also as a lesson to all succeeding generations, that crime should be properly punished. And it was no less a mercy to the sinners themselves that they should be cut short in their evil course. Had their life been spared, the same spirit that led them to rebel against God would have been manifested in hatred and strife among themselves, and they would eventually have destroyed one another. It was in love to the world, in love to Israel, and even to the transgressors, that crime was punished with swift and terrible severity" (*Patriarchs and Prophets*, pp. 325, 326).

A parable tells about a traveler who wanted to go through the Black Forest. In order to find his way he needed a guide. At the edge of the forest he encountered a hermit, who was willing to lead him to the other side. By the end of the first day's journey they came to a clearing and met a man who invited them to stay overnight in his home. "I'm so happy to have you come and rejoice with me," he said. "Today I was reconciled with my worst enemy, and to prove our reconciliation, he gave me this cup on the mantel."

As the hermit and traveler left the next morning, the hermit slipped the cup off the mantel and took it with them. The traveler asked, "Why did you do that?"

"I'm only doing as God does," the other said.

At the end of the second day they came to another clearing, where an evil, inhospitable man ordered them off his property. He had no time for them. They went on their way, but as they left, the hermit handed the first man's cup to him. "Why did you do that?" the traveler inquired.

"I'm only doing as God does," the hermit answered.

But at the end of the journey the hermit did something God doesn't always do: he explained his actions. The enemy of the first man had not made up with him. He had faked it and had given him a cup that had poison in it. So the hermit gave it to

Law and Gospel at Sinai

the man who needed a cup with poison. When the traveler heard the whole story, he could understand.

If we had sufficient information, we would be able to accept the blood and gore of the Old Testament a little better. All of God's reasons aren't apparent in every case, but we have received enough information to enable us to wait patiently to see more fully.

In the meantime we have evidences of mercy and forgiveness. After the slaughter of the three thousand, Moses went up into the mountain again, this time as an intercessor for the people.

One Friday afternoon as the sun set, Dr. Siegfried H. Horn and our group who were touring the Holy Land checked in at St. Catherine's Monastery at the foot of Mount Sinai. During our sundown worship on the flat roof outside, one of our group—a conference youth leader from the east coast—said, "I can never face my group of Pathfinders if I don't camp out overnight on top of Mount Sinai." He had hired a Bedouin guide by the name of Faraj, and three of us decided to go with him to the top of Sinai that night. It is a fearful trip up Mount Sinai after dark, particularly if you find yourself inescapably recalling all of the activity that has gone on up there.

We followed Faraj up the mountain to a place not far from the top called Wadi Musah, which means "the valley of Moses." That night we lay down with one sleeping bag among us, trying to keep warm. Although we left Faraj to forage for himself, he had a better plan than we did. In the middle of the night we woke up to find that the burning bush was back again. Faraj had brought matches with him, and in order to stay warm, he'd light a bush and curl around it. When that bush went out, he'd ignite another one. By the time the rest of the group arrived the next morning, Wadi Musah was blackened ruins.

From the Wadi Musah we went to the top of Safsaf, where we climbed through the cleft of the rock and looked down to the valley below in the wilderness of Sinai. Whether or not it's the same cleft where Moses hid from God's glory, only God knows.

But Moses spent forty days and forty nights somewhere on top of Sinai, and there he pleaded with God. How much time have we spent interceding with God for our loved ones, our friends, for church members, for stubborn people? How much time have we spent praying for those who would crush our heads if they got the chance? How much time have we spent for people whose hearts are still in Eygpt? Have we ever even prayed for one day, or one night? We can play or travel or talk all day, but what would it be like to pray all day? Moses did, for people who didn't even love him in return.

Exodus 32 pictures Moses as interceding with God. God had said, "I have seen this people, and, behold, it is a stiffnecked people: now therefore let me alone, that my wrath may wax hot against them, and that I may consume them: and I will make of thee a great nation" (verses 9, 10). "Moses, I'm sick

Law and Gospel at Sinai

and tired of these people. I'm going to start over with you!"

What would happen if God made that kind of offer to us today? to a person disgruntled with the church because some other member gave him a bad deal? Would we find it easy to say, "Now, God, you're really thinking. If You start over with me, You will have something worthwhile to build on." What if Moses had said, "This band of illiterate savages? Why, all they can think of are garlic and onions and fleshpots and Egypt. Now You're on the right track. Start over with me!"

Instead, Moses went to his knees and said, "Please, God, pardon these people. They have sinned greatly. Though they have made themselves gods of gold, forgive them." And he continued to implore God.

The evidence suggests that God didn't really intend to destroy them at that moment. When He said, "Let Me alone, Moses," what He really meant was, "Keep on, Moses. I need a human intercessor. Keep pleading." And God had a good intercessor in Moses. "Please, Lord, forgive these people their transgression, and if not . . . If not, then blot my name out of the book You have written."

Human beings have given their physical lives for others, but Moses was willing to exchange his eternal life for a people, who to all appearance, had no future. He pleaded for a people who had griped and complained, a people who had no time for him. But Moses knew that his name was in the book of life, and he was willing to throw it in the balance for them.

A person can get a love like that only one place—where Moses obtained it. The same man who directed in the punishment of the rebels was the one who interceded for the people who repented. An echo in advance, if you please, of Calvary, where Jesus said, "Father, forgive them; for they know not what they do" (Luke 23:34). No wonder Scripture links the name of Jesus and that of Moses throughout eternity.

The modern Advent movement had its Mount Sinai experience. Joseph Bates walked into the little town of Battle Creek and asked, "Who's the most honest man in town?" They notified him it was David Hewitt. Finding him, Joseph Bates told Hewitt the latest news was that the seventh day is the Sabbath. Hewitt *was* an honest man, and he accepted truth. The next time Bates came through town he baptized David Hewitt. And the word goes around. "The Advent people have come to Mount Sinai." We find the commandments of God, coupled with power from God to keep them. Grace is available at Sinai, not just law. God unfolded the gospel both to the Exodus generation and the disappointed people after 1844.

But God never gives His law apart from the gospel. He always presents the gospel as a solution of how to meet the law's demands. At Mount Sinai with the Exodus people, and in modern times with the Advent movement, the gospel unfolded in sandbox demonstration, in illustrated form that the people could understand. The sanctuary outlined

Law and Gospel at Sinai 55

the gospel for both those at Sinai and for those after 1844.

The Advent people encamped at their Mount Sinai for a time, as did the people of Israel, while they received further instruction. Then God spoke to them, "You have compassed this mountain long enough. Turn ye northward."

Chapter 6

When God Answered Prayer Against His Will

When people get tired of angels' food, is there something wrong with the food or with the people? "And the mixt multitude that was among them fell a lusting: and the children of Israel also wept again, and said, Who shall give us flesh to eat? We remember the fish, which we did eat in Egypt freely; the cucumbers, and the melons, and the leeks, and the onions, and the garlick: but now our soul is dried away: there is nothing at all, beside this manna, before our eyes" (Numbers 11:4-6).

God had finally told the people of Israel that they had lingered at Mount Sinai long enough. They moved forward, guided by the cloud, toward a place called Kadesh-barnea, approximately 150 miles from Sinai, right at the entrance of Canaan. The country there was desolate, "that great and terrible wilderness" (Deuteronomy 1:19). Before long the people began to gripe and complain.

Once again the mixed multitude started the trouble, this time muttering about the food. Perhaps they got tired of manna for breakfast and manna for dinner and manna baked and manna boiled and manna hot cakes and manna muffins. But it also involved something deeper.

A comment about manna for the Advent people today occurs in a book entitled *Medical Ministry:* "The light that God has given and will continue to give on the food question is to be to His people today what the manna was to the children of Israel. The manna fell from heaven, and the people were told to gather it, and prepare it to be eaten. So in the different countries of the world, light will be given to the Lord's people, and health foods suited to these countries will be prepared. . . . If we will come to the Lord in simplicity of mind, He will teach us how to prepare wholesome food free from the taint of flesh meat" (p. 267).

A lot of people in the Adventist faith have gotten nervous over the issue. In fact, we would have a division among us today if we talked very long about it, because according to the statistics and the surveys, we're just about 50-50 on vegetarianism. We don't believe in eating unclean meats—but vegetarianism, that's something else.

Some have told others that they cannot be good church members unless they quit eating meat. But when somebody tells you that you *have to do* something, how do you usually respond? I remember when I was a boy that we had to eat everything on our plates, and something of everything. It was with a great deal of gratitude that I scrapped that rule when I began my own home. It had caused a reverse reaction. If you want to be sure that your children will do something, tell them to do the opposite.

When I had a choice in the matter I discovered to my surprise that broccoli and cauliflower weren't that bad (expecially with mayonnaise). Born rebels, we don't like others to tell us what we must do. Many Adventists have gotten into a syndrome of feet-bracing against things involving diet. For that reason they have not been able to look at the situation objectively. But let's consider briefly some of the reasons God might have had for such instruction.

God didn't urge His people to turn away from certain things because He was trying to be nitpicky. Love motivated Him. The book *Counsels on Diet and Foods* says, "Cancers, tumors, and all inflammatory diseases are largely caused by meat eating. From the light God has given me, the prevalence of cancer and tumors is largely due to gross living on dead flesh" (p. 388). If you have studied anything at all about the batting average of the author of that book when it comes to predictions and analyses concerning health, sickness, and disease, then you have enough respect to take a long look at that kind of statement. When you examine it, you discover that it's not legalistic and nitpicking, but an evidence of God's love and concern for His people.

We can do what we want to with God's instructions. If we desire, we can even give stupid excuses. "It's just as bad to eat sugar!" Can you picture a group sitting around a table playing Russian roulette? Finally one of them exclaims, "Say,

When God Answered Prayer Against His Will   59

this is dangerous!" Another one retorts, "So what? So is skydiving!" And they keep on playing Russian roulette.

Eating of meat came only after sin, because flesh-eating requires death. God's kingdom to come will have no death. We also know that Jesus will not supernaturally change our tastes and desires and dietary habits when He returns. If I am accustomed to eating meat right up until then, I'm going to be looking for a butcher shop in heaven. All of a sudden it makes sense to learn that those translated to heaven without seeing death will have stopped the practice. If I'm going to live a certain way in heaven, it is reasonable for God to say, "As far as possible, do your best to live the same way now."

The children of Israel discovered that when they craved meat, God gave them what they wanted. "And there went forth a wind from the Lord, and brought quails from the sea, and let them fall by the camp, as it were a day's journey on this side, and as it were a day's journey on the other side, round about the camp, and as it were two cubits high upon the face of the earth. And the people stood up all that day, and all that night, and all the next day, and they gathered the quails: he that gathered least gathered ten homers: and they spread them all abroad for themselves round about the camp" (Numbers 11:31, 32).

Quail is clean meat. So the point here is not unclean meat at all. "And while the flesh was yet between their teeth, ere it was chewed, the wrath of the Lord was kindled against the people, and the Lord smote the people with a very great plague. And he called the name of that place Kibroth-hatavah: because there they buried the people that lusted" (verses 33, 34).

What was the issue? It wasn't a question of whether or not it was a sin to eat meat. Their problem was one of rebellion. When God gives me instruction and guides and clearly leads me in a certain way, but I brace my feet and say, "No thanks, I'm not interested," I display the real essence of all sin. It wasn't a question of whether or not they ate quail. The judgment came as a result of their rebellion against God.

Before they reached the borders of Canaan, another problem arose. Aaron and Miriam decided that they didn't like Moses as their leader. They began to criticize him, particularly for his Ethiopian wife. God responded by showing what a serious thing it is to find fault with His delegated leadership. Leprosy struck Miriam. And Moses, true to the heart that he had, went to his knees and pleaded in her behalf. Although healed in answer to his prayer, she had to remain outside the camp for seven days. The journey from Egypt to the Promised Land halted until the reinstatement of Miriam and Aaron.

Less than two years after leaving Egypt the people of God arrived on the borders of the land of Canaan. They came up with the idea, according to Deuteronomy 1:22, that they wanted to select a group of spies to go in and look over the land.

When God Answered Prayer Against His Will   61

Moses went along with it, and according to the record in Numbers, God Himself did too. It might appear at first glance that it was the Lord's idea, but it wasn't. God has always given His people the power of choice. And the remarkable thing is that He stays with them, sometimes in spite of what they choose.

The Hebrews selected twelve men to examine the land. They came back with their report. It was a good land, they unanimously agreed. But ten of the twelve said, "We can never go in. We aren't strong enough to take it." They were looking at themselves instead of to God.

While they discussed their discouragement, Caleb and Joshua jumped to their feet and began trying to share the enthusiasm that they felt. "Let us go up at once, and possess it; for we are well able to overcome it" (Numbers 13:30). But the ten said, "Oh, no. 'They are stronger than we, . . . men of a great stature. . . . We saw the giants, the sons of Anak, . . . and we were . . . as grasshoppers.' " And gradually the grasshopper complex spread among the congregation of Israel. They began to weep and to wail and to gripe again. "Wouldn't it be better for us to return to Egypt?" they said. They got together and appointed a pro-Egypt captain. The cry of the new movement was a terrible prayer that God would answer: "Would God that we had died in the wilderness. Would God that we had died in the wilderness."

Caleb and Joshua tried to stop the rebellion. "And they spake unto all the company of the chilren of Israel, saying, The land, which we passed through to search it, is an exceeding good land. If the Lord delight in us, then he will bring us into this land, and *give* it us; a land which floweth with milk and honey" (Numbers 14:7, 8).

But the people wouldn't listen to them. In fact, they decided that the thing to do was to stone them. "And the Lord spake unto Moses and unto Aaron, saying, How long shall I bear with this evil congregation, which murmur against me? I have heard the murmurings of the children of Israel, which they murmur against me. Say unto them, As truly as I live, saith the Lord, as ye have spoken in mine ears, so will I do to you: Your carcases shall fall in this wilderness; and all that were numbered of you, according to your whole number, from twenty years old and upward, which have murmured against me." "After the number of days in which ye searched the land, even forty days, each day for a year, shall ye bear your iniquities, and ye shall know my breach of promise" (Numbers 14:26-29, 34).

"Breach of promise"? Have you noticed that God's promises are often conditional? Jonah went to Nineveh and said, "In forty days Nineveh will be destroyed!" (Jonah 3:4, TEV*). But it was a conditional prediction. The people repented, and as a result God changed His decree about the city. Then you see Jonah sitting outside of the city, weeping and wanting to commit suicide because he was

---

*From The Bible in Today's English Version. Copyright, American Bible Society, 1976.

embarrassed. He said to God, "That's just what I thought You would do. You changed Your mind."

Scripture contains a number of conditional promises. This was one. God had promised to give the land of Canaan to the Exodus people. But they failed to go in by faith, and God had what appeared to be a "breach of promise." God gave them the sentence they had prayed for, that they would die in the wilderness.

"It was not the will of God that Israel should wander forty years in the wilderness; He desired to lead them directly to the land of Canaan and establish them there, a holy, happy people. But 'they could not enter in because of unbelief.' Hebrews 3:19. Because of their backsliding and apostasy they perished in the desert, and others were raised up to enter the Promised Land" (*The Great Controversy*, p. 458).

It is interesting to note that God did fulfill His ultimate plans. It was not a different movement that went into the Promised Land forty years later but simply another generation. "In like manner, it was not the will of God that the coming of Christ should be so long delayed and His people should remain so many years in this world of sin and sorrow. But unbelief separated them from God" (*ibid.*).

The unbelief manifested at Kadesh-barnea, which resulted in the people of Israel not occupying the Promised Land at that time, we see repeated in the history of the Advent people. We have had *our* Kadesh-barneas when the time was ripe and God tried to get the message through to us to go in to the heavenly Canaan. But because of our unbelief we could not and did not enter. "Every failure on the part of the children of God is due to their lack of faith" *(Patriarchs and Prophets,* p. 657).

We will study the modern counterpart of the Kadesh-barnea experience in the next chapter. But the interesting thing here is that when the people received the sentence that they must die in the wilderness they then had a reverse reaction, another example of the workings of "reverse psychology." When God told the people to go, they refused. But when He said, "I'll let you die in the wilderness as you have requested," they immediately decided to storm Canaan.

"And Moses told these sayings unto all the children of Israel: and the people mourned greatly. And they rose up early in the morning, and gat them into the top of the mountain, saying, Lo, we be here, and will go up unto the place which the Lord hath promised: for we have sinned" (Numbers 14:39, 40). It looked like repentance.

But "Moses said, Wherefore now do ye transgress the commandment of the Lord? but it shall not prosper. Go not up, for the Lord is not among you; that ye be not smitten before your enemies. . . . But they presumed to go up: . . . nevertheless the ark of the covenant of the Lord, and Moses, departed not out of the camp. Then the Amalekites came down, and the Canaanites which dwelt in that hill, and smote them, and discomfited them, even unto Hormah" (Numbers 14:41-45). And the people—the ones that came back—returned, licking their wounds.

It was no longer God's will for the people to go into the Promised Land, and when they tried to, they couldn't.

Here we come to a fantastic demonstration of the love of God. We see a people bruised and bleeding, discouraged and weeping. God answered their prayer against His will, and they were left with only one option: to accept their decision to return to the wilderness. But Moses and Aaron, Caleb and Joshua, go back to the desert with them. And above it all, the cloud guides them still.

It must have broken Moses' heart. He had already spent forty years in the wilderness learning *his* lesson. Now he must spend another forty years while the people learned theirs. But he went. Moses loved the people who did not love him, again demonstrating the eternal love of God. Do you think that God's love and patience are real? How easy it would have been for God to let all of us go, to blot the one world of sin out of existence. But God is merciful, and He still loves you and me today, still patiently tries to teach us the lessons of faith and trust that seem so hard to learn.

Chapter 7

We Are Still Here

Against His will God answered Israel's prayer, allowing all those who were twenty years old and above to perish in the wilderness, as they had requested. Forty years passed before the Exodus people again heard the call to go into the Promised Land.

One of the reasons for our study of the parallels between the Exodus and Advent people is to discover why we're still here. Hebrews 3:15-19 states, "To day if ye will hear his voice, harden not your hearts, as in the provocation. For some, when they had heard, did provoke: howbeit not all that came out of Egypt by Moses. But with whom was he grieved forty years? was it not with them that had sinned, whose carcases fell in the wilderness? And to whom sware he that they should not enter into his rest, but to them that believed not? So we see that they could not enter in because of unbelief."

This passage makes it quite clear that the people of Israel could not enter into the Promised Land as God had planned because of their unbelief. All of our failures, as individuals, or as a church, result from our lack of faith (*Patriarchs and Prophets*, p. 657). It isn't God's fault that we're still here, nor that of some leaders of our church. We are still here because of us. While it is probably cheap comfort, the Advent people are not the only ones who haven't had the faith to go into the Promised Land. They have had plenty of company, because no one else in the Christian world has had enough faith either. We are *all* still here.

"Let us therefore fear, lest, a promise being left us of entering into his rest, any of you should seem to come short of it" (Hebrews 4:1). When Paul talks about entering into God's rest, he's quoting from Psalm 95, and he is also referring, deliberately or unintentionally, to the words of Jesus in Matthew 11:28: "Come unto me, all ye that labour and are heavy laden, and I will give you rest." Notice that we are thinking of rest in two ways. First, individually: ceasing from our own works to get us to heaven, entering into His invitation to rest in His accomplished and completed work. Second, there comes a point historically when the body of Christ, His people, must enter into God's rest. Then will follow the entrance into the heavenly kingdom, the heavenly Canaan.

"For unto us was the gospel preached, as well as unto them" (verse 2). Paul here refers to the people of Israel going from Egypt to the Promised Land. "But the word preached did not profit them, not being mixed with faith in them that heard it. For we which have believed do enter into rest." If we have the experience of faith, of relationship with God, we enter into rest here and now, individually.

In verse 4 Paul connects this rest to the experience of the Sabbath: "For he spake in a certain place of the seventh day on this wise, And God did rest the seventh day from all his works." The Sabbath thus becomes an illustration of the experience of the genuine Christian.

"Seeing therefore it remaineth that some must enter therein, and they to whom it was first preached entered not in because of unbelief. . . . There remaineth therefore a rest to the people of God" (verses 6-9). It's encouraging to know that Scripture still calls individuals who haven't entered into His rest the people of God. What is this rest? It is not talking about ceasing from works, but rather resting from *my own* works. so it's possible to be still trying to get to heaven by our own works and be classed among God's people.

But God has something better that He wants us to understand. "For he that is entered into his rest, he also hath ceased from his own works, as God did from his. Let us labour therefore [the Christian must do something] to enter into that rest, lest any man fall after the same example of unbelief" (verses 10, 11). Here we see what the journey from Egypt to Canaan, from Babylon to the heavenly country, is about—entering into His rest, ceasing from our own works, accepting God's promises by faith, which will result in our entering into the heavenly kingdom at Jesus' coming.

So the effort that we need to put forth is to enter into rest, to cease from our own efforts to do what

God alone can do.

Let's take a little closer look at the Advent people following their great disappointment. The difficulty in recording the history of the Advent people during the years following 1844 is not one of lack of information but rather one of limiting the vast amount of information to fit into one chapter. (Those who would like to do further study on the subject should read *Christ Our Righteousness,* by A. G. Daniells, and the last half of the book *Selected Messages,* Book One).

The 1844 movement consisted of different types of people from various backgrounds. No Seventh-day Adventists existed by that name. That didn't come until the 1860s. People of all denominations listened to the call of over three thousand preachers of the prophetic message, proclaiming that Christ would return in 1844. They were correct in their interpretation of the time element, but they made one mistake in regard to what would occur at that time. However, as they discovered in their later study, although Christ did not intend to return in the fall of 1844, He had intended to come soon afterward.

Following the disappointment, thousands of people turned their backs on the movement and either became nominal Christians or left the church altogether. A handful of people continued to search and to study, to maintain a deep relationship with God, until they discovered truths that they hadn't noticed before and became excited about teaching and preaching and sharing what the Spirit unfolded to them.

Apparently it wasn't long, however, until they began to be more concerned about the work of the Lord than they were about the Lord of the work. They lost sight of Christ as the central focus of their messages and became argumentative and debative. Early in the 1850s Ellen White's messages to the church indicated concern over the trend: "Many have for years made no advancement in knowledge and true holiness. They are spiritual dwarfs. Instead of going forward to perfection, they are going back to the darkness and bondage of Egypt" (*Testimonies*, Vol. 2, p. 124).

Other typical comments written to the group of believers in those earlier days stated, "As a people we are not advancing in spirituality as we near the end." "My heart aches day after day and night after night for our churches. Many are progressing, but in the back track" (*ibid.*, Vol. 5, pp. 11, 93).

As early as the 1850s the Advent people were described as being lukewarm, neither cold nor hot. God began to send warnings to them to turn them from the direction they were headed and to help them see the difference between simply being religious—being promoters for the organization—or being spiritual and knowing God one to one.

In ancient Israel, when they refused because of their lack of faith to enter the Promised Land, they had only one option, to head back toward Egypt. The Advent people made the same choice. "Pride, covetousness, and love of the world have lived in the heart without fear of banishment or condemnation. Grievous and presumptuous sins have dwelt among us. And yet the general opinion is that the church is flourishing and that peace and spiritual prosperity are in all her borders. The church has turned back from following Christ her Leader and is steadily retreating toward Egypt" (*ibid.*, p. 217).

Warnings and counsel continued to come to the Advent people. At the end of the 1880s there began an increased interest in the subject of righteousness by faith in Jesus. God evidently was leading the Advent movement once more to the borders of the Promised Land. We find comments like these directed to the church at that time. "We are now upon the very borders of the eternal world" (*ibid.*, Vol. 4, p. 306). "The end of all things is at hand" (*ibid.*, Vol. 5. p. 16). "We are standing, as it were, on the borders of the eternal world" (*ibid.*, p. 382). "Eternity stretches before us. The curtain is about to be lifted" (*ibid.*, p. 464).

In 1888 the famous General Conference convened in Minneapolis. A ministerial institute preceding the General Conference studied the great theme of righteousness by faith in Jesus. Two men led in the meeting—one of them a gangly, rough, handlebar-moustached man from the army by the name of A. T. Jones; the other, more polished, careful in his theological works, was E. J. Waggoner. According to the historical records that we have, the discussions at Minneapolis became complicated by personalities, tempers, and divisions. In her final address, the last day of the meetings,

Ellen White said, "Now our meeting is drawing to a close. . . . There has not been a single break so as to let the Spirit of God in" (*Captains of the Host*, p. 594).

"An unwillingness to yield up preconceived opinions, and to accept this truth, lay at the foundation of a large share of the opposition manifested at Minneapolis against the Lord's message through Brethren [E. J.] Waggoner and [A. T.] Jones. By exciting that opposition Satan succeeded in shutting away from our people, in a great measure, the special power of the Holy Spirit that God longed to impart to them. The enemy prevented them from obtaining that efficiency which might have been theirs in carrying the truth to the world, as the apostles proclaimed it after the day of Pentecost. The light that is to lighten the whole earth with its glory was resisted, and by the action of our own brethren has been in a great degree kept away from the world" (*Selected Messages*, Book One, pp. 234, 235).

But a revival followed in spite of Minneapolis. The church witnessed repentances and confessions, and during the 1890s the message, backed solidly by the little woman who wrote the many books, moved forward among the Advent people. Notice the following comment in *Testimonies to Ministers*, pages 91 and 92: "The Lord in His great mercy sent a most precious message to His people through Elders Waggoner and Jones. This message was to bring more prominently before the world the uplifted Saviour, the sacrifice for the sins of the whole world. It presented justification through faith in the Surety; it invited the people to receive the righteousness of Christ, which is made manifest in obedience to all the commandments of God. Many had lost sight of Jesus. They needed to have their eyes directed to His divine person, His merits, and His changeless love for the human family. All power is given into His hands, that He may dispense rich gifts unto men, imparting the priceless gift of His own righteousness to the helpless human agent. This is the message that God commanded to be given to the world. It is the third angel's message, which is to be proclaimed with a loud voice, and attended with the outpouring of His Spirit in large measure."

What is the "third angel's message"? As the emphasis upon the theme of salvation through faith in Christ alone began to rise, a number of people had written to Ellen White and had evidently asked, "Is justification by faith the third angel's message?"

She replied in *The Review and Herald* of April 1, 1890, declaring, "Several have written to me, inquiring if the message of justification by faith is the third angel's message, and I have answered, 'It is the third angel's message in verity.' "

So the third angel's message is that Christ is our righteousness. In fact, righteousness by faith in Christ is the *beginning* of the loud cry, its *content*, and the *conclusion* of the loud cry of the latter rain.

Therefore the evidence is that the loud cry and the latter rain, the finish of God's work, began during those times when God brought us to the peak of emphasis about Jesus as our only hope. In 1892 she said, "The time of test is just upon us, for the loud cry of the third angel has already begun in the revelation of the righteousness of Christ, the sin-pardoning Redeemer. This is the beginning of the light of the angel whose glory shall fill the whole earth" (*Selected Messages*, Book One, p. 363).

Whenever the message of Jesus and our hope of salvation in Jesus alone begins to rise, you will know that the latter rain and the loud cry are upon us. But the question here is, If the loud cry began in 1888, can it go on for seventy, eighty, ninety years? We face only one conclusion. If the loud cry began at the end of the last century, something happened to it, or we wouldn't still be here. And what we're suggesting on the basis of our authority is that we had our opportunity to enter the Promised Land, but we turned it down and headed back into the wilderness.

The book *Christ Our Righteousness* records a meeting held in 1889 in South Lancaster, Massachusetts: "I have never seen a revival work go forward with such thoroughness, and yet remain so free from all undue excitement. There was no urging or inviting. The people were not called forward, but there was a solemn realization that Christ came not to call the righteous, but sinners, to repentance. . . . We seemed to breathe in the very atmosphere of heaven. Angels were indeed hovering around. . . . There were many who testified that as the searching truths had been presented, they had been convicted in the light of the law as transgressors. They had been trusting to their own righteousness. Now they saw it as filthy rags, in comparison with the righteousness of Christ, which is alone acceptable to God. While they had not been open transgressors, they saw themselves depraved and degraded in heart. They had substituted other gods in the place of their heavenly Father. They had struggled to refrain from sin, but had trusted in their own strength. We should go to Jesus just as we are, confessing our sins, and cast our helpless souls upon our compassionate Redeemer" (pp. 46, 47).

This is still His invitation. Are you on speaking terms with Him today? Have you learned to stop trying to resist evil yourself and turn your battles over to God? Do you know what it means not to rely upon your own achievement, performance, and good behavior for your hope of salvation? Have you entered into His rest?

At the beginning of the 1890s we were told, "For nearly two years we have been urging the people to come up and accept the light and the truth concerning the righteousness of Christ, and they do not know whether to come and take hold of this precious truth or not. They are bound about with their own ideas. They do not let the Saviour in" (*The Review and Herald*, March 11, 1890). A month later she reported, "Some of our brethren are not receiving the message of God upon this subject. They appear to be anxious that none of our ministers shall depart from their former manner of teaching the good old doctrines" (*ibid.*, April 1, 1890).

In the May 27, 1890, issue she declared, "God has sent to his people testimonies of truth and righteousness. . . . Those whom God has sent with a message are only men, but what is the character of the message which they bear? Will you dare to turn from, or make light of, the warnings, because God did not consult you as to what would be preferred? . . . Some have turned from the message of the righteousness of Christ to criticise the men and their imperfections."

A religious person who is not spiritual, until he *is* spiritual, will always brace his feet when others discuss spiritual things. Wouldn't it be safe to say that the religious person would become more nervous than even the nonreligious, because the former has thought that he had everything straight already. So spiritual things present more of a threat to him even than to one who has never claimed to know anything about God. That's why some of the cruelest persecutions in the past have come from people who have been the greatest religious people. Religious bigots, they couldn't stand the thought that after all their religiosity, they still didn't have true religion.

But they disguise their fear in various ways. For example, they may criticize those who bring the new insight, as some did in the 1890s. Or they may do their best to bring up some side issue to divert the discussion. Religious people who are not spiritual are quite comfortable discussing religious facts, but when others speak of the things that come the closest to the human heart, they can't stand it.

I was teaching a class on the life of Christ, and I made a prediction, just to warn the students, that when the time came to study the cross, some in the class would bring up any number of other topics instead. In spite of my warning, when we got to Gethsemane and the cross, it happened. Only a few students were awake and saw it happening.

"Some of our brethren have expressed fears that we shall dwell too much upon the subject of justification by faith, but I hope and pray that none will be needlessly alarmed; for there is no danger in presenting this doctrine as it is set forth in the Scriptures. If there had not been a remissness in the past to properly instruct the people of God, there would not now be a necessity of calling special attention to it" (*Selected Messages*, Book One, p. 372, written in 1890). "Do not allow your minds to be diverted from the all-important theme of the righteousness of Christ. . . . We want to keep the mind steadfastly to the point for which we are working" (*Christ Our Righteousness*, p. 92).

As the message of the 1890s began to get off the ground, some accepted it; others rejected it. And some, halfway in between, simply felt confused. Evidently they were unwilling to study it out for themselves. As a result, the whole issue began to get cloudy.

Even though a few talked and taught and studied the subject, gradually it faded away. And that is the only explanation of why we're still here. Because if we had continued to emphasize Christ as our only hope of salvation, this great theme, the loud cry, the latter rain, would have come to its fullness. God's work would have been finished. Christ would have returned, and some of us would never have been born.

Now let's notice some of the evidence that the emphasis on this message gradually began to ebb. "We may have to remain here in this world because of insubordination many more years, as did the children of Israel" (*Evangelism*, p. 696, written in 1901). In *The General Conference Bulletin* of March 30, 1903, Ellen White declared, "Brethren and sisters, from the light given me, I know that if the people of God had preserved a living connection with Him, if they had obeyed His Word, they would today be in the heavenly Canaan."

Earlier, in 1898, she said, "Had the purpose of God been carried out by His people in giving to the world the message of mercy, Christ would, ere this, have come to the earth, and the saints would have received their welcome into the city of God" (*Testimonies*, Vol. 6, p. 450).

In 1892 Ellen White wrote almost a prophecy of what would happen during the next few years. "No one can tell how much may be at stake when neglecting to comply with the call of the Spirit of God. The time will come when they will be willing to do anything and everything possible in order to have a chance of hearing the call which they rejected at Minneapolis" (from a letter to Ole A. Olsen, General Conference president, dated September 1, 1892).

Looking back after some years had passed, denominational historian Arthur W. Spalding wrote, "Without a doubt the fathers of the Second Advent cause believed in the atoning grace of Christ as the sole means of salvation. It was acknowledged by Andrews, Waggoner, Smith, Loughborough, Cottrell, James White. And perhaps every member said amen. Yet, because in the minds of most the doctrine was assumed as the basic truth rather than emphasized as the dominant truth, it was in a great measure lost sight of" (*Captains of the Host*, p. 587).

Surveys indicate that only one out of four church members today spends any time at all in a daily, continuing, private, personal communication with Jesus. It would be safe to say that we have assumed too much by concluding that everybody knows that Christ alone is the basis of our salvation. Wouldn't it be correct to say that if I don't have any time to experience a constant one-to-one relationship with Jesus by taking time alone in comtemplation of the life of Christ and in prayer—If I don't have any time for that, even though I might believe theoretically that Christ is the only hope of salvation—I am still a victim of Babylon or Egypt, and I still need to wake up to the message of righteousness by faith?

How did the church arrive at its present situation? " ' Surely, Christ saves us,' " many argue, " 'but whoever knowingly breaks the Sabbath cannot be saved.' " But Spalding calls such an idea "a half truth on an unsound base." He explains, "The implication was that whoever observed the seventh day as the Sabbath thereby earned a part of his salvation; therefore, it was by his works that he was saved—with the help of Christ." And then he concludes, "True enough, Sabbathbreaking is an evidence of unregeneracy; but the unregeneracy comes before the Sabbathbreaking, and it is the state of unregeneracy, rather than its works, which prevents salvation. The unregenerate man has no power to keep the law. He must first receive Christ; he will then be a new man, and the keeping of the law will follow. For the reception of Christ's love and life within the soul inclines and enables man to keep the law of God, including the fourth commandment. He is not saved because he keeps the Sabbath; he keeps the Sabbath because he is saved; and Sabbathkeeping is more than observing the day" (*ibid.*).

The vividness of their feeling for truth at times led Jones and Waggoner to meet the opposition with extreme statements that shut out works altogether from the experience of the Christian, as though faith could live and not work. In fact, one time Jones said, "Works amount to nothing. We are saved by faith alone." And he got a letter from Ellen White, who said, "I know your meaning, but you leave a wrong impression upon many minds" (*Selected Messages*, Book One, p. 377).

Another problem was that the men, sharing human infirmities, sometimes failed to show the humility and the love that righteousness by faith imparts. This has been one of the problems of offshoots. Many groups have split off from the

Seventh-day Adventist denomination over the issue of righteousness by faith. Getting all excited about the theory, they say, "This is what the church needs." So they begin to shout it from the housetops. And if anyone questions them or in any way doubts what they're saying, they lop off his head with their ecclesiastical sword. "What's the matter with you?" they shout. "Don't you understand that righteousness is by faith?" It would be like shouting at your wife, "What we need around here is more love!" By your very attitude you would have negated and canceled out the message that you were trying to proclaim.

It happened in the days of Luther. Some of the peasants and laymen, excited about Luther's message, said, "Luther is right." Then they went out and began to throw rocks through church windows and to topple images. Luther went to his knees and said, "Lord, deliver me from my friends!"

One of the most tragic things that has happened in the emphasis in all ages upon righteousness by faith is that a person can get enthusiastic about the theory ahead of experiencing the relationship with Jesus that it talks about. The theory of righteousness by faith is a dangerous weapon in the hands of one who is a victim of that problem.

This conflict neither originated in the 1880s nor concluded in the 1890s. It continues today.

The parable of the ten virgins takes on a new meaning when we specifically apply it to those who live just before Jesus comes. All ten of them slumbered and slept. "While the bridegroom tarried, they *all* slumbered and slept" (Matthew 25:5). How could the five wise virgins doze and still be ready when the bridegroom came? I'd like to propose to you that they slept for reasons beyond their control.

When God told the children of Israel that their prayer had been answered, that all of the people twenty years and older who had left Egypt would die in the wilderness, and that they would wander there for forty years, what happened to the people under twenty? Why did *they* wander in the wilderness? I want to suggest that it is possible in the history of the Advent movement that we have had a period of wilderness wandering for reasons initially beyond our control. But there arrives a time when God once more urges, "Go in and possess the Promised Land."

Not until the end of the wilderness wandering did the message come again that was designed to take the Exodus people into the earthly Canaan. But all that time God stayed with them, led them, called them His people. I'm thankful for a God of love who manifested that love to the people of Israel and who is still demonstrating it to His people today.

Chapter 8

Sleeping in the Wilderness

The children of Israel refused to go into the Promised Land, and so they remained in the desert for forty years. The reason they couldn't go in earlier was because of their lack of faith, resulting from the absence of a faith relationship. We can apply the situation personally as well as corporately. Wilderness is the product of unbelief. The Promised Land results from faith. It's just that simple.

Now let's consider something that happened just after the people of Israel failed to enter the Promised Land and headed back toward the wilderness, because we find a parallel in the modern Advent movement as well. The Hebrews' first reaction was to weep and to wail and to apparently repent because of the judgment. A group tried to storm Canaan and to take it by their own strength. Moses warned them not to. Significantly, those who tried to conquer Canaan broke away from the main body of God's people and became, so to speak, an offshoot group. They attempted to do themselves, on their own, what only God could have accomplished. Consequently they came back bruised and bleeding.

Then another faction tried the same thing, only using different techniques. A man named Korah and two of his friends, Dathan and Abiram, led it. Instead of submitting to exile, they said, "Moses has taken too much on himself. Everybody is holy. Who does he think he is?" Korah and his companions began a new movement designed to overthrow God's appointed leadership and to go to Canaan on their own. He flattered Israel that the fault was with the leaders, not with the people. He maintained that the people were holy, and under the right leadership "they would proceed directly to the Promised Land" (*Patriarchs and Prophets*, p. 398). But the nation's acceptance of Korah and his companions provided another evidence of Israel's lack of faith. Once God told them to return to the wilderness, anyone who departed from the pillar of cloud, the leadership of God and His chosen representative Moses, exhibited a lack of faith.

Numbers 16 tells how the whole thing turned out. The earth swallowed up Korah, Dathan, and Abiram. Fire destroyed 250 princes, and 14,700 laymen died in a plague.

The modern Advent movement has experienced a number of splinter movements, many of them on the basis of righteousness by faith, but all of them with the idea that there's something wrong with the church, the leadership, and the body of believers. "We've got to change it," they said. "Let's pull away from the church. Let's go into the Promised Land.' If you've studied any of our history, you're familiar with such movements.

In *Testimonies to Ministers* (pp. 32-62), Ellen White warns against the whole concept of the church's becoming Babylon, that the only way to get to the Promised Land is to separate from the church and start your own movement. The thirty pages are quite clear on the subject. "The church of Christ on earth will be imperfect, but God does not destroy His church because of its imperfection" (*ibid.*, p. 46). "The tares and the wheat are to grow together until the harvest; and the harvest is the end of probationary time. . . . False brethren will be found in the church till the close of time" (*Christ's Object Lessons*, pp. 72, 73). "The church may appear as about to fall, but it does not fall. It remains, while the sinners in Zion will be sifted out" (*Selected Messages*, Book Two, p. 380).

What church is the book talking about? The organic church—the denominational organization —or the mystical church, those who know Christ and who love God wherever they are? The statement that the church is about to fall would have to be talking about the organic church. The mystical body of Christ, those who follow Him and who are His saints everywhere, would not be about to fall. "The church . . . remains, while the sinners in Zion will be sifted out—the chaff separated from the precious wheat. This is a terrible ordeal, but nevertheless it must take place. None but those who have been overcoming by the blood of the Lamb and by the word of their testimony will be found with the loyal and true, without spot or stain of sin, without guile in their mouths. We must be divested of our self-righteousness and arrayed in the righteousness of Christ."

So in the Advent experience, as well as in the Exodus, the same movement that started from Egypt goes into the Promised Land. A different generation, yes, but the same movement. We observe all kinds of evidences against offshoots and splinter groups as we study both the Exodus and Advent movements.

Sacramento, California, was the headquarters of a group who desired to clean up the church. Pastoring in the city at the time, we had a chance to get acquainted with their activities. The movement had begun in Europe during World War I. Apparently it started over the issue of whether or not to bear arms in Germany. But after the war, when our world organization was able to try to get things back together, they refused to come back. They had gotten a taste of power and wanted to clean up the whole church. But they began to have trouble within their own ranks. An older pioneer who came from Europe to our country told me that one time the group met in their union session. In the morning they disfellowshiped the president of their union, but in the afternoon of the same session they reinstated him into the church fellowship and made him president of the division.

The leadership later transferred to the United States. Some of the reformers decided they'd better reform the reformers who were trying to reform the church. So there were reformers who were reforming the reformers.

One day R. L. Benton, an Adventist preacher who was one of a kind, found himself in Sacramento with a few hours to spare during a weekend trip. He decided to drop in the headquarters of the reform movement. The son of its world president was there and invited him to stay for dinner and sundown worship. As they began to eat, the son, who was also a minister, began to unload on Elder Benton all of the things that were wrong with the Seventh-day Adventist Church. He listed them on and on while Benton just listened. After the younger man had run down, Elder Benton said, "Son, I'm old enough to be your grandfather. Isn't that right?"

The younger man nodded. "Yes."

"I knew all these things were wrong with the church before you were born," Benton continued.

"You did?"

"Yes. Do you know what your problem is? You're trying to clean the house from the outside. Anybody knows you've got to be inside the house to clean house." At that point things got kind of quiet around there.

Let's admit that the organic church has plenty of problems. But the only way they will receive any help is for us to stay inside and try to correct them.

John 12:40 says that God blinded the eyes and hardened the hearts of those who did not believe. And 2 Corinthians 4:3, declares, "But if our gospel be hid, it is hid to them that are lost: in whom the god of this world hath blinded the minds of them which believe not, lest the light of the glorious gospel of Christ, who is the image of God, should shine unto them."

One part of the Bible states that God blinded the eyes of those who did not believe, and another part tells us that the devil blinded those who did not believe. Now who did it? God or the devil? or the people themselves? And what was the blindness?

Selected Messages, Book One, p. 239, comments, "The Jews refused to accept Christ as the Messiah, and they cannot see that their ceremonies are meaningless, that the sacrifices and offerings have lost their significance. The veil drawn *by themselves* in stubborn unbelief is still before their minds. It would be removed if they would accept Christ, the righteousness of the law.

"Many in the Christian world also have a veil before their eyes and heart. . . . Heavy is the veil that darkens their understanding. The hearts of many are at war with God. . . . They may talk of Christ as their Saviour; but He will finally say to them, I know you not." (emphasis supplied).

The sun shines on two different objects, wax and clay. It melts the wax and hardens the clay.

Scripture says that God hardened Pharaoh's heart. How did he? By commanding that his heart be hard? By removing Pharaoh's choice? No, by letting the sun shine on Pharaoh's heart, which was clay.

Tragedy strikes two different families in the church, both apparently Christians. One shakes its fists at God. "If that's the way You're going to treat us, forget it!" Its members are clay. The other lifts up its eyes to heaven and says, ' "The Lord gave, and the Lord hath taken away; blessed be the name of the Lord.' " This family is wax. All that God does is to *reveal* the kind of material we're made of. At the same time the devil struggles to get us to remain clay, instead of becoming wax.

One hopes that many of those people who wandered around in the wilderness, before their families buried them in the desert sands, found hearts of flesh, hearts of wax.

As the people roamed the desert their number must have increased. But at the same time the population of the Promised Land, where the giants lived, also rose. As one preacher once said, "Those giant women were giving birth to fifty-pound babies!" The population explosion went on in the land of Canaan, as well as in the wilderness.

Does an increase in numbers represent success? The modern Advent movement can easily deceive itself on this point. It is possible for a church to pat itself on the back because its statistical reports through the years have always continued to rise. We can trick ourselves into thinking that because our numbers are growing we are really succeeding, thus mistaking quantity for quality. "If numbers were evidence of success, Satan might claim the pre-eminence; for in this world his followers are largely in the majority. It is the degree of moral power . . . that is a test of . . . prosperity. It is the virtue, intelligence, and piety of the people composing our churches, not their numbers, that should be a source of joy and thankfulness" (*Testimonies*, Vol. 5, pp. 31, 32).

We can become drunk with success based on the latest miracle reports. It's too bad that we spend our time counting Israel when we should spend our time weighing Israel. If, instead of congratulating ourselves for our statistical reports compared with last year or with the beginning of our history, we would get a glimpse of what might have been, it would drive us to our knees.

In *Christian Service* [1903], page 268, Mrs. White wrote, "The Lord is good. He is merciful and tender-hearted. He is acquainted with every one of His children. He knows just what each one of us is doing. He knows just how much credit to give to each one. Will you not lay down your credit list and your condemnation list, and leave God to do His own work? You will be given the crown of glory if you will attend to the work that God has given you."

We must do away with credit lists, with praising ourselves for our achievements! *We are still here!*

Something else happened during the wilderness wandering. "During these years the people were constantly reminded that they were under the divine rebuke" (*Patriarchs and Prophets*, p. 406). God told them to discontinue the rite of circumcision, which had been a distinct sign of the separateness of God's people. They had to stop celebrating the Passover. "The wilderness wandering was not only ordained as a judgment upon the rebels and mur-

Sleeping In the Wilderness

murers, but it was to serve as a discipline for the rising generation, preparatory to their entrance into the Promised Land" (*ibid.*, p. 407).

We noticed that the ten virgins can all slumber and five of them still be ready to go in when the bridegroom comes. Evidently it is because they slept for reasons initially beyond their understanding or choice. But it's possible to doze for your own reasons, as well as for those of your forefathers, and we've probably had plenty of that. But those who were twenty years old and under, who went through the wilderness because of the lack of the faith of their fathers, evidently acquired from their fathers their own lack of faith. Is it possible for this to happen today?

Have you ever heard from childhood up, "You'd better be good. If you're good, then Jesus will love you" or "You'd better do what's right. If you do what's right, then you'll go to heaven"? Is it possible that some of the people in the wilderness taught some of their children the wrong things? Their idea of faith was that you must have works as the *cause* of your entrance in the Promised Land. They evidently believed that faith plus works was the way to get to heaven, instead of salvation by faith alone. And what resulted from such thinking? The only records of their wilderness life are instances of rebellion against the Lord.

What are the possible causes of this? Alternative No. 1, Did God do this to them? Did He say, "You have failed. Now you're going to have to burn in the desert for forty years!" Is that the loving God that Jesus clearly presented in His life here on earth?

Alternative No. 2. Did God announce that they would have to remain in the desert for forty years because He knew that it would take them that long before some would have enough faith to enter Canaan?

Or did God's foreknowledge realize that it would be forty years before some other condition reached its fulfillment? If you've studied Deuteronomy already, you probably realize that the people who finally went into the Promised Land entered in spite of the whole group, not because of it. It wasn't because they had done anything to merit it or because the movement *as a whole* had found enough faith to enter in.

In Deuteronomy 9:4-8 Moses talks to the people who finally stand on the borders of the Promised Land. He reviews their past history. "Speak not thou in thine heart, after that the Lord thy God hath cast them out from before thee, saying, For my righteousness the Lord hath brought me in to possess this land: but for the wickedness of these nations the Lord doth drive them out from before thee" (verse 4). Then, in case someone wasn't listening, he repeats, "Not for thy righteousness, or for the uprightness of thine heart, doth thou go to possess their land: but for the wickedness of these nations the Lord thy God doth drive them out from before thee, and that he may perform the word which the Lord sware unto thy fathers, Abraham, Isaac, and Jacob. Understand therefore, that the

Sleeping In the Wilderness

Lord thy God giveth thee not this good land to possess it for thy righteousness; for thou art a stiffnecked people" (verses 5, 6).

Had they learned their lesson? "Remember, and forget not, how thou provokedst the Lord thy God to wrath in the wilderness: from the day that thou didst depart out of the land of Egypt, until ye came unto this place, ye have been rebellious against the Lord." "Ye have been rebellious against the Lord from the day that I knew you" (verses 7, 24). Now Moses approaches the end of his speech, and he begins to feel the breath of death. "For I know thy rebellion, and thy stiff neck: behold, while I am yet alive with you this day, ye have been rebellious against the Lord; and how much more after my death?" (Deuteronomy 31:27).

Because of God's foreknowledge, He knew that the people *as a whole* would not succeed where their forefathers had failed. Also He knew that the heathen nations of the land of Canaan would fill up their cup of iniquity in forty years. Then God would call an end to the whole thing for that reason. He would take those people left after the mighty shaking across the Jordan into the Promised Land.

What's our conclusion in the Advent movement? It's obvious that we failed to enter in because of unbelief. In spite of those times when God gave the signal and appealed mightily to our hearts, we went back into the wilderness. We have wandered for many years, and during that time, many of us have been more or less blind.

" 'The false ideas that were largely developed at

Minneapolis have not been entirely uprooted from some minds. Those who have not made thorough work of repentance under the light God has been pleased to give his people since that time, will not see things clearly, and will be ready to call the messages God sends, a delusion.' "

Some who refused to accept the experience of faith would call righteousness by faith a delusion: " 'There are those who have prided themselves on their great caution in receiving "new light," as they term it; but they are *blinded* by the enemy, and cannot discern the works and ways of God. . . . They set up false standards' " (*General Conference Bulletin*, 1893, pp. 184, 182). And then in a remarkable letter written to Dr. Magan, December 7, 1901, Mrs. White observes, "A few who may now seek to bridge the gulf that stands so offensively before God must make haste slowly or else the standard bearers will fall, and who will take their place?"

As you look back on the history of the Advent movement since the turn of the century, you can almost count on your fingers the names that have prominently championed salvation by faith in Christ alone. Of the standard-bearers before the turn of the century, at least five stand out: Jones, Waggoner, Ballenger, Chadwick, and Luther Warren. Four of the five left the church.

And of course some people began to judge the message that they taught on the basis of whether they stayed or apostatized. And so you have the interesting counsel that the few who would like "to bridge the gulf" "must make haste slowly," . . .

Sleeping In the Wilderness

until the end of the wilderness wanderings. But in the desert the people heard God's voice declaring, "Ye have compassed this mountain long enough. Turn ye northward."

God comes to the point in the history of each movement when He says, "I'm going to use ways and means by which you will see that I'm taking the reins in my own hands. The simple means He uses to bring about and perfect His work in righteousness will surprise His people.

I sat down recently and went through the Bible and the index to the writings of Ellen White, and I found practically nothing that even suggested that *man* is going to "finish the work." That phrase is our own invention. It is almost traditional among us. "Let us arise and finish the work!" I don't believe that God's work is going to be completed until He says so, and that will happen when the nations of the earth have filled up their cup (Revelation 11:18). Then those who love God with all their hearts will be involved with Him in the finishing of the gospel proclamation as He takes control. And it won't be because some supersalesman managed to give them some kind of guilt complex about not witnessing. It will be because they have an experience with Jesus that is so overwhelming that they can't keep quiet.

Isn't it time we got on our knees before God and said, "Lord we have tried hard. But we have not succeeded, and we never will. Our only hope is in Your doing the work. Make us willing to let You control and guide us."

"With unerring accuracy the Infinite One still keeps an account with all nations. While His mercy is tendered, with calls to repentance, this account will remain open; but when the figures reach a certain amount which God has fixed, the ministry of His wrath commences. The account is closed. Divine patience ceases" (*Testimonies*, Vol. 5, p. 208). God has a point past which our world goes on no longer.

But God's mercy for His erring children extends to this day. The patience and love He had for the Exodus people, in spite of the fact that "their heart was not right with him, neither were they stedfast in his covenant" is still available to us today. For "he, being full of compassion, forgave their iniquity, and destroyed them not: yea, many a time turned he his anger away, and did not stir up all his wrath. For he remembered that they were but flesh; a wind that passeth away, and cometh not again" (Psalm 78:37-39). "Like as a father pitieth his children, so the Lord pitieth them that fear him. For he knoweth our frame; he remembereth that we are dust' (Psalm 103:13, 14).

Chapter 9

Striking the Rock, With Moses

"Then came the children of Israel, even the whole congregation, into the desert of Zin in the first month: and the people abode in Kadesh; and Miriam died there, and was buried there" (Numbers 20:1).

The Bible record of people who fell asleep is quite short. You don't see long processions like we witness today with great men of state. Just the simple statement. Perhaps it has significance for us today.

"And there was no water for the congregation: and they gathered themselves together against Moses and against Aaron. And the people chode with Moses, and spake, saying, Would God that we had died when our brethren died before the Lord!" (verses 2, 3). The reference here is to the death of Korah, Dathan, and Abiram. A terrible attitude for people who stood on the borders of the Promised Land, it provides more evidence that the generation from which came the people of Israel who finally crossed the borders of Canaan had no more faith than the one that had failed to enter there forty years before.

"And why have ye brought up the congregation of the Lord into this wilderness, that we and our cattle should die there? And wherefore have ye made us to come up out of Egypt, to bring us in unto this evil place? it is no place of seed, or of figs, or of vines, or of pomegranates; neither is there any water to drink" (verses 4, 5).

As you study the story you discover that the ceasing of the flow of water was one of the greatest signs that the people could have had that their wilderness pilgrimage was just about over. God had supplied them with water out of dry ground and out of the rocks. It had started at Rephidim before they got to Sinai and continued all through their desert journeying. It wasn't the same rock as at Rephidim, but it was water gushing out where they needed it most. Wherever they moved and set up camp, coming from the sands of the desert or from other rocks or rock clusters, the water was always there until they came near to the close of their exile. Then it ceased. It should have been a mighty indication that they were about to claim the Promised Land, where there was plenty of water, and they would no longer need such a miracle. Unfortunately, it depends on whose glasses you look through—those of faith or those of distrust—as to what you do with the evidence of the nearness of the Promised Land.

One person hears about some tremendous event that has taken place, and he gets panicky and fearful. Another learns of some sign of the nearness

Striking the Rock, With Moses

of Christ's return, and he lifts up his head and rejoices. Two people called me on the day the Supreme Court ruled Sunday blue laws constitutional. One cried, "Isn't it terrible?" The other said, "Isn't it wonderful?" You can know pretty well which side you are on by your reaction. Do you get panicky, or do you say, "Thank You, Lord; it's almost here."

The people griped and complained because they had no water. They couldn't see anything positive whatsoever in the sign. Moses and Aaron went from the presence of the assembly to the door of the tabernacle of the congregation. They fell on their faces, and the glory of the Lord appeared to them. "And the Lord spake unto Moses, saying, Take the rod, and gather thou the assembly together, thou, and Aaron thy brother, and speak ye unto the rock before their eyes: and it shall give forth his water, and thou shalt bring forth to them water out of the rock: so thou shalt give the congregation and their beasts drink. And Moses took the rod from before the Lord, as he commanded him. And Moses and Aaron gathered the congregation together before the rock, and he said unto them, "Hear now, ye rebels . . ." (verses 7-10). Strange words coming from one who was known as the meekest man in all the earth. Moses had been an impatient man: He had taken the Egyptian's life and fled Pharoah. Forty years of sheepherding had taught him meekness over that. But for a moment he lost his hold upon God, and his natural impatience again surfaced.

"Hear now, ye rebels." Were they rebels? Yes, but he was saying the right thing in the wrong spirit. It is one thing to say the truth but another to proclaim it in the wrong spirit. How many of us have been guilty of that in our families, with our children? "Hear now, ye rebels; must *we* fetch you water out of this rock? [Catch the key words, "must *we*."] And Moses lifted up his hand, and with his rod he smote the rock twice: and the water came out abundantly, and the congregation drank, and their beasts also" (verses 10, 11).

Here you have another experience of God answering prayer against His will. In the first place, He did not desire that they get water out of the rock again. That is why He had cut off the supply. In the second place, it wasn't His will to bring water out of the rock through the method that Moses used. But it still happened. The water came in spite of Moses, not because of him. The person who approaches God with the wrong method will sometimes get the right results at the moment. But not later. God will sometimes reward wrong methods with right results because of the honor and vindication of His name.

Moses erred in several ways. First, truth is not to be spoken in passion. Second, he showed a distrust of God when he asked the question, "Must we bring forth water?" Third, he assumed power that belongs only to God when he said, "Must *we* bring water out of this rock?" He knew it wasn't *we* but only God. It doesn't say whether Moses employed "we" to indicate him and Aaron. That would have

Striking the Rock, With Moses

been a gross error for Moses and Aaron to assume the prerogatives of God, an echo of the devil's first deception in the Garden of Eden. "You don't need to rely on God," Satan implied; "you can do it yourself." On the other hand, Moses may have meant something else, something that at first glance looks much better. When Moses said "we," he may have referred to himself and God, sort of a cooperation agreement. "God will do part of it, and I will do part of it. Must God and I bring forth water out of this rock?"

Right here you run into a mistaken understanding of the principle of cooperation. I would like to take the position that man's power plus God's equals no power. The only thing that God had asked Moses to do was speak to the rock. What would we call speaking to the rock today? Do you recall who the Rock is? "They drank of that spiritual Rock that followed them: and that Rock was Christ" (1 Corinthians 10:4). Speaking to Christ, the Rock, is prayer.

Moses knew theoretically that he could not do anything, not even part of the task of bringing water out of the rock. God would have to do it all. Notice that it was during this particular experience that Moses operated under the delusion of distrust and passion and separation from God. Since every failure on the part of God's children results from their lack of faith, therefore Moses' faith must have grown thin and his trust in God wavered before this moment ever arrived. When you study the condition of Moses at the time, you discover that remorse and weariness over the long wilderness wandering had bogged him down. When it began to look like the people of the next generation weren't going to be ready to go in either, it was almost more than he could stand. It distracted his attention away from God to himself. We also have evidence that fear of the Amorites and the other heathen nations that they soon had to face began to disturb him. And he began to let go of his abiding dependence upon God. All of this set the stage for the episode of the rock.

Moses knew all the facts and theory. He recognized that he personally had had nothing to do with opening the Red Sea, that he did not bring the manna. As leader of the Hebrews, he had had experience after experience of total dependence upon God, learning that God did it all, and that all he could do was look to God for Him to do it.

But in spite of the fact that he knew the theory so well, there was something more important. Experientially Moses failed. As a result he began beating on the rock.

In the first place, he went beyond what God had asked him to do. It isn't God plus my efforts, but God alone. Second, the rock had already been struck. Christ is to be smitten only once: "Christ was once offered . . ." (Hebrews 9:28). Moses' act broke the symbolism that God had in mind. But above all, it involved man's assuming the place of God and then ascribing glory to himself, whether consciously or unconsciously. "Must *we* fetch you water?" When the water came, guess who would have gotten part of the glory? However, justification is "the work of God in laying the glory of man in the dust, and doing for man that which is not in his power to do for himself" (*Testimonies to Ministers*, p. 456).

You don't have to be in Moses' shoes to strike the rock. Peter wasn't. The disciples headed into the Garden. Peter has reserved for himself a sword, and when the mob came and the high priest's servant approached, Peter used it. He cut off the servant's ear. He struck the rock, with Moses. It happened to be an ear, but it was still the Rock. Jesus had promised to take care of His followers. He didn't need their help.

But the incident was only a prelude to what Peter did a little later. In Caiaphas' hall the guards pushed and hit Jesus. Again and again they struck Him. Then they threw an old coat over His head. Slapping Him, they demanded, "Prophesy who hit You, if You are a prophet." Snatching the coat off, they spit in His face and slapped Him again.

All the while Peter stood by the fire. Someone accused him of being a follower of Jesus. Peter was in trouble. He had a relationship with God but believed in God's power plus his effort. And so he began defending himself. The disciple thought that God helped those who help themselves. And he struck the rock, with Moses.

Peter didn't realize that the Rock he struck that night was the Stone which the builders rejected. "Save yourself. Do it yourself. Get out of this yourself." The apostle didn't believe in doing it *all* by himself. He had had a relationship with Jesus for some time, but experientially he struck the Rock. The worst blow that Jesus received that night was from him.

The problem goes clear back to the beginning of the human race. When Cain and Abel were told what to do when they came to worship God, Cain said, "I will do something myself." He brought the fruits of his own labors, the fruits of his own efforts, to present before God. He struck the rock, with Moses. It was not that he didn't believe in God. He came to worship and followed God's instruction—up to a point. But at that point *he* took over.

It has been the same issue down through the centuries. God has never promised to do certain things for us. But the things that He *has* said He will do for us He is able to accomplish. One of the things that God has vowed to do for us is to fight our battles against sin and Satan. "Man is not able to save himself, but the Son of God fights his battles for him, and places him on vantage-ground by giving him His divine attributes" (*Review and Herald*, February 8, 1898). The key is to know for certainty what God has promised and not to go one iota beyond trusting Him in prayer and faith on the things He has told us He will do for us.

So one of the big lessons at the rock in the wilderness was the lesson of "cooperation," where it begins and ends.

The water that came forth from the rock also represents Christ. "In the last day, that great day of

Striking the Rock, With Moses

the feast, Jesus stood and cried, saying, If any man thirst, let him come unto me and drink. He that believeth on me, as the scripture hath said, out of his belly shall flow rivers of living water. (But this spake he of the Spirit, which they that believe on him should receive)" (John 7:37-39).

All that we can do toward salvation from sin or sinning or a world of sin is to drink the water of life, through communion with Christ, in prayer and study of His Word (*Selected Messages*, Book One, p. 343; *Thoughts From the Mount of Blessing*, p. 113).

"And the Lord spake unto Moses and Aaron, Because ye believed me not, to sanctify me in the eyes of the children of Israel, therefore ye shall not bring this congregation into the land which I have given them" (Numbers 20:12). Can you imagine the feeling that must have come over Moses when he heard that?

For the first forty years of his life he had studied in the schools of Egypt and the military academy of Upper Egypt. Then, during the second forty years of his life, he had unlearned all of the wrong things that he had acquired in Egypt, primarily self-dependence. At the end of forty years in the wilderness by himself, the sheep had taught him the lesson of total dependence upon God, that he could do nothing of himself.

Then God took him down to Egypt against his personal preference, and Moses led Israel. But the Hebrews turned down the invitation to go into the Promised Land, and once again Moses faced forty years of wilderness exile. Eighty years of wandering in the desert. Day after day the big hope in his heart had been that some day those people who loved to gripe and complain would shout for joy when they arrived at the Promised Land and saw it flowing with milk and honey. It was the one thing that Moses had looked forward to—the gratitude and joy and excitement of that throng as they entered Canaan. And now he received word that he would not be able to accompany them.

Moses began to pray about it. It seemed almost more than he could bear. He pleaded with the Lord to allow him to go in. Finally God told him not to pray about it anymore. Evidently Moses had such a tug at God's heartstrings that God was afraid He would give in! Eventually Israel's leader surrendered to that lonely climb up Mount Nebo, where he died alone of a broken heart.

In the meantime Israel sent a message to the people in the land of Edom that the Hebrews wanted to go through. Here, in essence, you have the two brothers meeting again—the children of Jacob and the children of Esau. The descendants of Esau sent word back: "You are not coming through the land of Edom." Today a road called the king's highway goes through there. It travels between precipitous canyon walls and gorges and is a shortcut into Canaan. God planned for the children of Israel to pass through there. He would have influenced the Edomites to soften their hearts and allow the Hebrews to pass.

But the people of Israel did not have enough faith, and they turned away for the second time

Striking the Rock, With Moses

from the borders of the Promised Land. They began a detour around Edom that would last two years before they would come up for the last time to the borders of the Promised Land at another location.

"And the children of Israel, even the whole congregation, journeyed from Kadesh, and came unto mount Hor. And the Lord spake unto Moses and Aaron in mount Hor, by the coast of the land of Edom, saying, Aaron shall be gathered unto his people: for he shall not enter into the land which I have given unto the children of Israel, because ye rebelled against my word at the water of Meribah" (Numbers 20:22-24).

Of the four people left who had been above twenty years of age when they left Egypt—Moses, Aaron, Caleb, and Joshua—two would now die. Aaron was the first to go.

Three people climb up the side of Mount Hor: Moses, Aaron, and Eleazar, Aaron's son, who is to become priest in his father's stead. Can you imagine planning your own death and funeral, knowing the exact time? God said, "Go up the mountain, and there Aaron will die."

The people at the bottom of Mount Hor watch as three lonely figures leave the camp and start up the mountainside. They have some kind of insight into what's going to happen, knowing that Aaron will pass on his robes to Eleazar. Moses realizes that it won't be long until he will be going to sleep like Aaron. They must have talked and reminisced on their way up the mountainside, remembering the days in Egypt, years before, when Aaron and

Miriam had something to do with saving Moses in the bulrushes from Pharaoh. Perhaps they reminisced about the times they played on the banks of the Nile River. Surely they must have compared notes about the times when their paths had crossed, and all the joys and sorrows, failures and successes, disappointments and hopes, that they had gone through together. And they must have thought of the time at Mount Sinai when Aaron had really failed and built the golden calf. Maybe Aaron went to his knees once more and implored God's forgiveness. And so they walked up the side of the mountain.

Eventually they came to the top, and there we are told that Aaron died in the arms of Moses, his brother. Wouldn't you like to be somewhere in the throng, someday soon, when you see Moses and Aaron clasp each other once more?

According to the record, Moses took the robes, the priestly garments of Aaron, and put them on Eleazar. The two of them dug a grave and buried Aaron, and before long the congregation saw only two coming back down from Mount Hor.

The God of heaven and the angels looked on and beheld the scene. It must have wrung the heart of the Son of God with grief.

If we were to stop at the episode on Mount Hor, we might possibly have some doubts and questions. But that is not the end of the story. Our world is one of sin and unfairness, but God has never held us accountable for being born here. He has made provision for eternity, which will more than make up for the inconvenience of our birth here. Everyone has an adequate opportunity to accept God's plan. Aren't you thankful for the provision that He has made?

Chapter 10

You Don't Have To Know the Reason

The legalistic Christian in professed Christian churches usually asks the question, "What?"—what to do, what not to do. The student of world religions poses the question, "Which?" The eschatologist inquires, "When?" The righteousness by faith theorist asks, "How?" The righteousness by faith experientialist seeks the answer to, "Who?" And the intellectual wants to discover, "Why?"

Intellectuals apparently existed in the days of Moses. They demanded, *"Why* look at a snake?" And they perished with the comfort that although they were dying in agony, they were at least being "intellectually astute"!

The people of Israel began a detour around Edom that took two years. "And they journeyed from mount Hor by the way of the Red Sea, to compass the land of Edom: and the soul of the people was much discouraged because of the way. And the people spake against God, and against Moses, Wherefore have ye brought us up out of Egypt to die in the wilderness? for there is no

You Don't Have to Know the Reason

bread, neither is there any water; and our soul loatheth this light bread" (Numbers 21:4, 5). How often the griping started about the diet!

"And the Lord sent fiery serpents among the people, and they bit the people; and much people of Israel died. Therefore the people came to Moses, and said, We have sinned, for we have spoken against the Lord, and against thee; pray unto the Lord, that he take away the serpents from us. And Moses prayed for the people. And the Lord said unto Moses, Make thee a fiery serpent, and set it upon a pole: and it shall come to pass, that every one that is bitten, when he looketh upon it, shall live. And Moses made a serpent of brass, and put it upon a pole, and it came to pass, that if a serpent had bitten any man, when he beheld the serpent of brass, he lived" (verses 5-9).

Have you ever wondered what you would have done if you had been there? When I was small I thought it was foolish. Make a snake and put it on a pole? How can you get any sense out of that? I would like to point out that you don't have to know the reason. God is reasonable, and He is the One who invites us to "come now, and let us reason together." But have you ever noticed the rest of the verse? "Though your sins be as scarlet, they shall be as white as snow" (Isaiah 1:18). Some things God wants to us to understand and to reason out, while others are a waste of effort. Many highly intelligent people are smart except for one thing: They are not quite smart enough to realize how dumb they are!

The first thing we notice is that God sent the fiery serpents. Scripture also says that the Lord hardened Pharaoh's heart. Earlier we noticed *how* God did that—by letting him come into circumstances that revealed what kind of heart he already had. God has provided us enough evidence that we don't have to sit around blaming Him for being a vindictive God. Here is where we need to do a little thinking. What God has given us information on, we can reason about.

Herpetologists have done some studies in the Wilderness of Sin. They have discovered evidence that the snakes were there all the time. For almost forty years God had been protecting the Hebrews from the snakes. When they began to gripe and complain after their second denial of God's invitation to enter the Promised Land, He simply withdrew His protection for a while. God is not pushy—He doesn't even force His protection on anybody. And the devil was happy to do the job of getting all the snakes into one big mob. Enough snakes already lived there without God's creating more.

Suppose I choose to go skiing instead of going to church, and I break my leg. "I shouldn't have done this," I say later. "God broke my leg to punish me." But the Lord didn't break it. It's just that He won't push His protection on me.

"Well," you might say, "then it was an accident."

No, I think maybe the devil broke it. Because, first of all, Satan likes to break legs, and second, the

You Don't Have to Know the Reason

devil knows that I will likely blame God for it, and the devil likes nothing better than for us to blame God for tragedy. So I think he would be more than happy to do the job.

So it shows up in Scripture that the Lord sent the fiery serpents. The person already unfriendly to God will shake his fist at Him every time tragedy strikes. Someone already mad at God loves to take a passage like "the Lord sent fiery serpents" and picture in his imagination God on His throne exclaiming, "Look at those wretches down there! I'll fix them!" A crisis doesn't change us or our attitude toward God. It only reveals which way we were already thinking and gives us a big push in that same direction.

The serpents came and bit the people. "Much people . . . died," Scripture explains. "Now there was terror and confusion throughout the encampment. In almost every tent were the dying or the dead. None were secure. Often the silence of the night was broken by piercing cries that told of fresh victims" (*Patriarchs and Prophets*, p. 429). Imagine what that would have been like in the encampment of Israel.

God told Moses to get some brass and make a snake. It seems foolish. In the first place there wasn't time. How can you take time to fashion a metal snake when there are people crying for help? But Moses did as God said. He didn't sit there and ask, "Why? I don't get it, God. I don't understand. Give me some good reasons." He had learned that when God the Father speaks, there are times when you don't question Him.

A three-year-old sits in the backyard, playing. It starts to rain, and his mother leans out the door and calls, "Come in."

"Why?"

" 'Cause you'll get wet."

"Why?"

" 'Cause it's beginning to rain, and you'll catch a cold."

"Why?"

" 'Cause when you get wet and cold you get sick."

"Why?" By that time the child is soaked.

Another mother leans out the back door. "Come in."

"Why?"

"Because I said so."

Sometimes it is wise to obey and do what God says without asking questions. You don't have to know the reason. The issue is, Do you trust Him? Is God the kind of Person that you can trust? In a sense, the reason you ask the question why is because you don't trust Him. It is inherent in the question.

Moses didn't hesitate or protest. He got busy and made a snake out of brass. Paul gives us a possible reason why he fashioned a snake instead of a lamb to put on the cross. "For what the law could not do, in that it was weak through the flesh, God sending his own Son *in the likeness of sinful flesh*, and for sin, condemned sin in the flesh" (Romans 8:3). A serpent has always represented sin. The serpent on the cross symbolized Jesus, who came in the likeness of sin. He deals with the question why also in 2 Corinthians 5:21:

"For he hath made him to be sin for us, who knew no sin; that we might be made the righteousness of God in him." An interesting text to ponder, it talks about a trade. God made His Son to be sin for us. But that never made Him a sinner. The snake that Moses put on the cross had no poison in it. Jesus had no sin or guile in Him. But Jesus became sin for us, in our place on the cross, that we might be made the righteousness of God in Him. When we are made the righteousness of God in Him, that never makes *us* righteous. We are only righteous *in Him*. And we are not righteous any longer than we are in relationship with Him.

If a snake had bitten you in the middle of the night back there and you yelled for help, it would have been stupid to try to figure out why the snake, why not a lamb? The only wise thing would have been to do exactly as God had said—to trust Him.

Jesus brought up the story when He talked with Nicodemus. Just before that favorite Bible verse, John 3:16, you have Jesus' own reference: "As Moses lifted up the serpent in the wilderness, even so must the Son of man be lifted up: that whosoever believeth in him should not perish, but have eternal life" (John 3:14, 15).

In all ages since, people have said in one way or another, "Don't look at the snake. It's stupid to look at it." The evolutionist argues, "I cannot believe in Creation; it doesn't make sense. How could anyone create something in one day, when according to all human intelligence it would take long periods of time?" So the reasoning goes on, and the evolutionists end up with the comfortable realization that they came from a long process and that they have only threescore and ten years to live. And they die without any hope for eternity because they were being intellectual. But God tells me "that whosoever believeth in him should not perish, but have eternal life."

If some of the options that the skeptics and the cynics have brought up had anything to compare with eternal life, I might be more impressed. But their ideas are a literal dead end. The cross is foolishness to the worldly wise. But the worldly wise aren't smart enough to realize how dumb they are.

Someone else might protest, "I don't understand why one man can sin, and everyone else suffers because of his act. Therefore I am going to throw the Bible on the trash heap." Another complains, "It doesn't make any sense to say that one man can die for millions of people's sins." And so they scrap the whole thing. Trying to be wise, they are also being foolish. Just as foolish as the man who said, "I refuse to go out and look at the snake on the pole."

In the days of Noah the people came by and scoffed and made fun. "Who ever heard of a raindrop, let alone a flood?" But Noah kept building his ark, and the people asked, "Why?"

"Because a flood is coming."

You Don't Have to Know the Reason

"What's a flood?"

"I can't explain it to you until you see it. But get into the ark."

"Why?"

"Listen, antediluvians, you don't have to know the reason. You will find out soon enough!"

"But we want to know why."

Pseudointellectualism! Of course in those days scientists and the philosophers could explain everything, even as some "do" now. Even when the animals came, people stood there and wondered. Animals, birds, and creeping things entered the ark. Why? When people chose not to get on board the ark, they could always bolster their decision with an explanation by their smart men.

C. T. Everson pictured the scientist before the Flood explaining to the layman about the creeping things and the animals boarding the ark. "Why," he said, "this is simply 'an innate propulsion of the animal kingdom animated by the supreme activity of the subconscious mind and superinduced by posterior spheres of cerebral afterglow; sensitizing every scintilla of the corporeality of the brute creation, this effecting a translocation of their materialistic concepts to more salubrious environments' "

The layman stands there, nods his head, and says, "Oh, of course. I hadn't thought about that." He trusts the big man, the smart man. The scientist knows why because he has been to the university. They go down in the Flood, but they had the assurance that they had been intellectually sophisticated.

God warns Nebuchadnezzar, "Please don't walk on your veranda and say, 'Isn't this great Babylon that *I* have built?' You are going to lose your mind some day."

"But why?"

"Because of self-glorification and pride—a part of Babylon."

"Why? Why? Why?" And Nebuchadnezzar does lose his mind one day. But God is merciful and gracious to him. The day comes when the king wakes up and acknowledges the great God of heaven and admits that he himself is only a creature. He stops asking so many *whys*.

Jesus takes mud and pastes it on a blind man's eyes. Skeptics of the Bible, even sometimes religionists sitting in the church, demand, "Why?" Then some try to come up with all kinds of mud compresses and health remedies and naturopath theories. I don't know why Jesus used the mud or what kind it was. If I have chosen to look at God askance, through skeptical eyes, I could exclaim, "That's stupid; that's foolish." But you don't have to know the reason. The truth is, the man went and washed in the pool of Siloam, as Jesus had told him, and he came away seeing. The other people standing around asked, "Why?" He said, "I have no idea. All I know is that where before I was blind, now I can see."

The prophet tells Naaman to go and wash in the dirty river. Naaman has clear rivers in his own land. "Wash in the dirty river seven times? Why?"

You Don't Have to Know the Reason

(Don't look at the snake.) But his counselors prevailed, and Naaman did as they urged him. He came away cleansed from the leprosy.

Someone hears about the relationship between smoking and lung cancer and questions, "Why?" The intellectual, the one who doesn't do anything unless he knows all the reasons why, proclaims, "Any coward can give up smoking. It takes a real man to face lung cancer!" A young person hears that if he takes drugs and continues to play around with them, he is going to make oatmeal out of his brain. "Why? I don't understand. It's fun." (Don't look at the snake. It's stupid to look at snakes.) He destroys himself, and he finds his answer, but it's too late.

Two young people don't believe that God means what he says about fornication and adultery. "We live in a different world now. Don't swallow what your father and mother say. It doesn't make any difference now." But God declares, "Don't do it." They persist, "Why? Why?" Thousands of broken hearts have awakened too late with the realization that you don't have to know the reason.

Two young people decide they want to get married. Father and mother, who know them best, tell them they aren't ready. He doesn't have a job. She doesn't know how to keep a home. They are simply not responsible or mature. The preacher tells them the same thing. "Why?" You don't have to know all the reasons, because you would not be able to understand all of it anyway. Can you trust God and

His counselors? your parents, who have been loyal to you up to this point? Again and again we fall into the ranks of those people who sat in their tents and refused to go out and look because they couldn't understand the reason.

"Many are unwilling to accept of Christ until the whole mystery of the plan of salvation shall be made plain to them. They refuse the look of faith, although they see that thousands have looked, and have felt the efficacy of looking, to the cross of Christ. Many wander in the mazes of philosophy, in search of reasons and evidence which they will never find, while they reject the evidence which God has been pleased to give. They refuse to walk in the light of the Sun of Righteousness, until the reason of its shining shall be explained. All who persist in this course will fail to come to a knowledge of the truth.

"God will never remove every occasion for doubt. He gives suffcent evidence on which to base faith, and if this is not accepted, the mind is left in darkness. If those who were bitten by the serpents had stopped to doubt and question before they would consent to look, they would have perished. It is our duty, first, to look; and the look of faith will give us life" (*Patriarchs and Prophets*, p. 432).

Will you accept God's friendly invitation? To understand, yes, just as much as He has chosen to reveal. But beyond that, to admit that you don't have to know the reason, only to trust Him.

Chapter 11

So Near
And Yet So Far

For the third time the children of Israel reached the borders of the Promised Land at the Jordan River. According to the Book of Deuteronomy, though, as a group they had not changed that much. Many of them were still far from Canaan in heart and outlook. But the nations of the heathen had filled up their cup of iniquity. God shook out the people who did not have the faith to go in and took the ones who did across the Jordan.

The reason we finally enter the heavenly country will not be because we as a group of a few million have changed that much. It will be because the nations of the world have filled up their cup of iniquity, and God will take into the heavenly country those who have the faith to go in. The rest get shaken out. So if you have been waiting around for several million people to reproduce the character of God, don't hold your breath. On the basis of this study, I believe that Jesus is coming very soon, whether the entire church is ready or not.

"And the children of Israel set forward, and pitched in the plains of Moab on this side Jordan by

Jericho. And Balak the son of Zippor saw all that Israel had done to the Amorites." Balak got nervous because the Amorites had overcome the Moabites. King of the Moabites, Balak figured that if the Israelites defeated the Amorites, who had already conquered his country, they were in deep trouble. He reasoned there was no point in trying to fight. So he came up with a bright idea. He would have them cursed.

"And Moab said unto the elders of Midian, Now shall this company lick up all that are round about us, as the ox licketh up the grass of the field. And Balak the son of Zippor was king of the Moabites at the time. He sent messengers therefore unto Balaam the son of Beor to Pethor, which is by the river of the land of the children of his people, to call him, saying, Behold, there is a people come out from Egypt: behold, they cover the face of the earth, and they abide over against me: come now therefore, I pray thee, curse me this people; for they are too mighty for me: peradventure I shall prevail, that we may smite them, and that I may drive them out of the Land: for I wot that he whom thou blessest is blessed, and he whom thou cursest is cursed" (Numbers 22:1, 2, 4-6). Evidently Balaam had a reputation as having a rather effective curse.

"God said unto Balaam, Thou shalt not go with them; thou shalt not curse the people: for they are blessed" (verse 12). Whatever God blesses, no one can curse. So Balaam told the messengers what the Lord had said. Balak, however, was persistent. "And Balak sent yet again princes, more, and more

So Near and Yet So Far

honourable than they" (verse 15). So the VIPs visited Balaam and begged him again to come and curse Israel. "And God came unto Balaam at night, and said unto him, If the men come to call thee, rise up, and go with them; but yet the word which I shall say unto thee, that shalt thou do. And Balaam rose up in the morning, and saddled his ass, and went with the princes of Moab" (verses 20, 21).

Now we encounter the familiar story that shows up in all of the children's books—the tale of Balaam and the donkey. The donkey saw the angel of the Lord, and even donkeys know how to respect the angel of the Lord. Balaam was so blind that he couldn't see it. He struck the animal because of its apparent obstinance and refusal to go straight ahead. After the donkey crushed his foot against the wall at the gate, Balaam again beat it unmercifully.

"And the Lord opened the mouth of the ass, and she said unto Balaam, What have I done unto thee, that thou hast smitten me these three times? And Balaam said unto the ass, Because thou hast mocked me: I would there were a sword in mine hand, for now would I kill thee. And the ass said unto Balaam, Am I not thine ass, upon which thou hast ridden ever since I was thine unto this day? was I ever wont to do so unto thee? And he said, Nay" (verses 28-30).

Can you imagine a man dialoguing with a donkey without even being startled? He should have fallen off the donkey in surprise. But instead, he was so upset that he could go ahead and talk with the animal as though this were a regular, everyday happening. It shows how angry a man can get and also how determined he can be to achieve his own ends. Persistent and rebellious, he vowed to get his own way regardless.

Then the Lord opened Balaam's eyes. He saw the angel of the Lord in his path, his sword drawn. But in spite of all the evidence, Balaam said, "If it displease thee, I will get me back again" (verse 34). "*If* it displease thee"!

"Go ahead," the angel said, "but remember that you will have to say what I tell you."

Balaam arrived at Balak's palace, and the next day the Moabite king took him out to the top of the high place of Baal, overlooking the camp of Israel, Balaam went through his ceremonial rituals there. Apparently they resembled the sacrifices of God's people. Then he began to try to curse Israel. "How shall I curse, whom God hath not cursed? or how shall I defy, whom the Lord hath not defied? . . . Let me die the death of the righteous, and let my last end be like his!" (Numbers 23:8-10).

"I beg your pardon," Balak said. "I brought you out here to curse these people, and you have blessed them." So Balaam had to remind Balak that he could say only what God told him.

"Let's try again," Balak urged. "We will go to another spot." So they went to the top of Mount Pisgah. From there they could see only a part of Israel's encampment. He hoped that their numbers would not be so impressive and perhaps he could curse them one group at a time. Again Balaam went through his ritual. Then he began, "God is not a man, that he should lie; neither the son of man, that he should repent: hath he said, and shall he not do it? or hath he spoken, and shall he not make it good? Behold, I have received commandment to bless: and he hath blessed; and I cannot reverse it" (verses 19, 20).

A strange statement appears in verse 21: "He [God] hath not beheld iniquity in Jacob, neither hath he seen perverseness in Israel." But at that moment down in the camp of Israel lived at least twenty-four thousand people doomed to die in the next few days because of their iniquity and perverseness. Was God blind? Didn't He see those twenty-four thousand? Or up to a point does God, in His kindness and love, look at the body of His people through the glasses of the merits of Jesus? Evidently we have had some evidence of that in our own past history. In spite of rebels, lack of belief, and wandering in a spiritual wilderness, we hear that the church is still "the only object on earth on which Christ bestows His supreme regard" (*Selected Messages*, Book Two, p. 396).

Balaam continued blessing the people until finally the Moabite leader ordered him to stop. "It would be better for you to stop right here while we are still ahead," he said essentially, "or at least before we get further behind! Don't say anything more."

But then Balak foolishly decided to try one more time. They went to the top of Peor and went through their ceremonies a final time. "How goodly are thy tents, O Jacob, and thy tabernacles, O Israel! . . ." Balaam said. "God brought him forth out of Egypt; he hath as it were the strength of an unicorn: he shall eat up the nations his enemies, and shall break their bones, and pierce them through with his arrows. . . . Blessed is he that blesseth thee, and cursed is he that curseth thee."

"And Balak's anger was kindled against Balaam. [Do you blame him?] And he smote his hands together: and Balak said unto Balaam, I called thee to curse mine enemies, and, behold, thou hast altogether blessed them these three times. Therefore now flee thou to thy place" (Numbers 24:5-11) In other words, "Get out of here! Go home!"

But as Balaam leaves, of all things, he shouts another blessing over his shoulder. It contains what many consider to be one of the most interesting predictions of the coming of the Messiah in all Scripture: "I shall see him, but not now: I shall behold him, but not nigh: there shall come a Star out of Jacob, and a Sceptre shall rise out of Israel, and shall smite the corners of Moab, and destroy all the children of Sheth" (verse 17).

Balaam went home licking his wounds because of his damaged ego. He had hoped to get riches and honor, and all he got was Balak's displeasure. As a result, Balak, tugging on his beard and scratching his head, began to pace on his plush carpets in his palace and wonder what he should do next. He is not big enough to fight. His idea to curse his enemies had gone sour. What would happen now?

So Near and Yet So Far

But Balaam had still not given up. Remembering some of the reasons why God's people were blessed, as he stared at his ceiling, trying to think what to do, Balaam came up with a bright idea. You will find the suggestion of his strategy in the book *Patriarchs and Prophets*. Balaam showed up again at Balak's palace. "The reason that these people are blessed," he said, "is because of their allegiance to the God of heaven, because of their obedience. Now if you can in some way get them to break their allegiance and obedience, no one will have to curse them for you. The curse will be automatic."

Liking the sound of Balaam's suggestions, Balak asked him for ideas. Balaam had some. He suggested, since the women of Moab were known to be among the most attractive of women, that Balak pick the most beautiful among them and send them over to the camp of Israel. Really listening now, Balak planned a party with Balaam and invited the Israelites. Twenty-four thousand went, many of them leaders in Israel. The party was a tremendous success—from Balak's point of view.

One of the strange things about his experience is that Moses evidently didn't see what was happening. What happened to him? He could tell what was going on in the plains below from the top of Mount Sinai and knew what was happening when the people danced around the golden calf. Moses had had access to the Urim and Thummim through Aaron and Eleazar. And yet he didn't know what was going on until the apostasy became practically national. Evidently God allows some of His leaders to be blind for a time for some purpose.

Someone gave me a little formula one time. I have used it many times since. It has no mathematical logic, but it makes sense. They said, "If something goes wrong, don't forget T over O."

"What's T/O?" I said.

"In God's *Time* and on His *Occasion* He will make things right."

Things work out in God's time and on His occasion. If you have seen wrong in the church, at headquarters, among leaders, God knows about it. Though some will seem blind to it for a while, God takes care of things in the end.

Eventually Moses learned that "Israel joined himself unto Baal-peor: and the anger of the Lord was kindled against Israel. And the Lord said unto Moses, Take all the heads of the people, and hang them up before the Lord against the sun, that the fierce anger of the Lord may be turned away from Israel. And Moses said unto the judges of Israel, Slay ye every one his men that were joined unto Baal-peor" (Numbers 25:3-5). Twenty-four thousand people lost their lives in the hangings, the slaughter, and the plague that broke out.

One of the princes of Israel, Zimri by name, came back from the party at Peor, and he had a Moabite prostitute with him. Going through the camp, right in front of Moses and the people who mourned for the apostasy, he took her into his tent (Numbers 25:6). A son of Eleazar, Phinehas, couldn't take it, and evidently moved by God, he grabbed his javelin and followed Zimri and the prostitute into the tent and nailed them both to the ground with his javelin.

Some people today try to picture such a God of love that never hurts anybody. "The earthquake just happened to come at the proper time with Korah, Dathan, and Abiram. Everything just happened naturally." No, God *is* a God of love, but He is *also* a God of justice, and we had better never forget that. People ultimately destroy themselves in the end because their attitude and rebellion is their choice. But let's not say that He has nothing to do with its happening. As a result of Phinehas's act, he was honored with the priesthood in his family forever.

Finally the sifting and the shaking and the reorganization of the lines in Israel there on the banks of the Jordan ended. Eleazar, Phinehas's father, asked to number Israel, counted them up, and discovered that everyone twenty years old and upward who had left Egypt was gone—except Caleb, Joshua, and Moses—just as God had predicted years before. "But among these there was not a man of them whom Moses and Aaron the priest numbered, when they numbered the children of Israel in the wilderness of Sinai. For the Lord had said of them, They shall surely die in the wilderness. And there was not left a man of them, save Caleb the son of Jephunneh, and Joshua the son of Nun" (Numbers 26:64, 65).

In the early Advent movement, people made fun and scoffed. After the Great Disappointment they said, "Well, we thought you people had your ascension robes ready and were going to go up. But you're still with us. Isn't that interesting? How come you didn't go up?" They laughed and ridiculed and cursed. But cursing hurts only the feelings. It has only given publicity. Even the blood of the martyrs was the seed of the gospel. Smart people don't curse, knowing they only help the cause of the underdog.

Giavanni Popinne wrote a book with the premise that we are too hard on the devil, that if we would stop attacking him, we would have less people interested in him, because the masses tend to be sympathetic toward the underdog. Perhaps his idea has some truth to it. "There are Christians who think and speak altogether too much about the power of Satan. They think of their adversary, they pray about him, they talk about him, and he looms up greater and greater in their imagination" (*The Desire of Ages*, p. 493).

I remember going to Michigan with my preacher father and uncle when I was a boy. They opened up their evangelistic meetings in a large hall in downtown Grand Rapids. Quite a group of people sat on the front row the first night. We found out later what had brought them there. Some pastor in a large church in town, feeling threatened by the meetings, had stated in his church that if any of his members went to hear them, they would be disfellowshiped from the church. As a result a large crowd attended the first night.

At a camp meeting in the Northwest several years ago, some people against the church distributed leaflets. Our leaders got up in camp meeting and said, "Whatever you do, don't read this material. Go home and burn it!" And I knew people who went home and pulled it out of their wastebaskets to read it just because of the warning.

When you see a sign along the side of the highway that says, "Don't read the other side of this sign," everybody in the car turns around to read it. The devil knows reverse psychology. After he has cursed for a while, and tried to downgrade and ridicule, he will reverse his tactics. Sometimes he switches them overnight. First he led people to curse Israel: Next he suggested, "Be friendly. Invite them to a party." It worked beautifully.

What do we have today? The ecumenical movement urges us to be friends, to bury our differences. We're all brothers, and everybody is going to the same place. All roads lead to the same kingdom. The enemy reverses his tactics.

We have plenty of evidence that the church will face a heavy inroad of immorality just before Jesus comes. But the only people who become involved in it are those who trust to themselves instead of to the Lord Jesus Christ.

In Bible prophecy a woman represents a church. In Revelation a pure woman symbolizes a pure church; a fallen or corrupt woman, a fallen, corrupt church. So if the Exodus movement parallels the Advent people, then in a prophetic sense you could have the women of Moab symbolizing the heathen, or fallen, churches. Babylon consists of fallen churches. Have you seen the fraternization with the women of Moab in the prophetic, spiritual sense as well as the literal? Look for both interpretations. We have observed some already, and we may witness a whole lot more before we're finished.

What we really see on the borders of the Promised Land is a mighty sifting and shaking taking place. God seeks to separate His people from the world. Satan tries to lead God's people away from Him, for the curse is always automatic when that happens. It never fails. I'm not sure that I feel at the moment like joining Phinehas with his javelin, but I would like to be on the side that Phinehas represents. I want to be among those who are more concerned with the character and the glory of God than they are with anything else.

Chapter 12

The Mighty Shaking

According to the third chapter of Revelation, up until shortly before Jesus comes, the world contains three groups. "And unto the angel of the church of the Laodiceans write; These things saith the Amen, the faithful and true witness, the beginning of the creation of God" (verse 14). And here begins what we call the Laodicean message. The Laodicean message has two parts. Part 1 we find in verses 15-17: "I know thy works, that thou art neither cold nor hot: I would thou wert cold or hot. So then because thou art lukewarm, and neither cold nor hot, I will spue thee out of my mouth. Because thou sayest, I am rich, and increased with goods, and have need of nothing; and knowest not that thou art wretched, and miserable, and poor, and blind, and naked."

May I suggest that we label the first part "The Rebuke to Laodicea." God says, "You are wretched, miserable, poor, blind, naked." God never leaves us, however, in rebuke or reproof without helping us to know what to do about the problem. So verse 18 starts Part 2: "I *counsel* thee to buy of me gold tried in the fire, that thou mayest be rich; and white raiment, that thou mayest be clothed, and that the shame of thy nakedness do not appear; and anoint thine eyes with eyesalve, that thou mayest see."

"I counsel thee to buy of me gold tried in the fire." The gold represents faith and love. "And white raiment, that thou mayest be clothed." The white raiment stands for Christ's garment of righteousness. "And anoint thine eyes with eyesalve, that thou mayest see." We understand the eyesalve to depict spiritual discernment that comes as a result of the activity of the Holy Spirit. The Holy Spirit gives us spiritual eyesight.

So verse 18, the Part 2 of the Laodicean message, we could label as "The Counsel." "I *counsel* thee . . ." Remember, Part 1 is "The Rebuke" and Part 2 is "The Counsel."

Interestingly enough, verse 19 gives both of them in one verse: "As many as I love, I rebuke and chasten" (Part 1). "Be zealous therefore, and repent" (Part 2).

We have noticed in the Laodicean message three groups of people: the hot, the cold, and the lukewarm. But when Jesus comes there are just two.

So the big question is, "What happens to the third group?" God brings rewards only for the righteous and the wicked—also called the sheep and the goats, the wheat and the tares, the good and the bad, the just and the unjust. But we do not read of any lukewarm reward for the lukewarm. They disappear from the scene.

I believe that today we stand on the banks of the Jordan River, in the midst of a shaking and sifting just as the Exodus people experienced prior to their crossing over into the Promised Land.

Do you know what causes this lukewarm condition? At home we have a single-spout faucet in the kitchen. On each side is a handle. The left side is hot, the right one is cold. Now, in order to get lukewarm, you turn on some of each. Lukewarmness comes as a result of combining hot and cold.

The evidence in Matthew 23 is that such people mirror those who lived in the days of Christ's first advent. They are hot on the outside but cold on the inside. In other words, they have hot works but cold hearts. Their works and behavior look good. They appear to be good moral people. What they lack, however, is the proper motivation from within. Suffering spiritual schizophrenia, they are two people in one, acting one way and being another way inside. That's what makes them lukewarm. But they disappear. God has to spew them out.

What determines whether a person is really hot or cold? In Matthew 7 and Matthew 25 it's quite obvious that the dividing point is whether or not people know God. "Depart from me. *I never knew you.*"

"Oh, but we've done many wonderful works. We've cast out devils . . ."

"I never knew you."

"Your eternal destiny is *based* not upon your

works but upon *whom you know*. Without question, that is the teaching of Scripture. Jesus said in His prayer in John 17, "This is life eternal, that they might know thee the only true God, and Jesus Christ, whom thou hast sent."

One group consists of those who know a living relationship with the Lord Jesus Christ. As a result they have on Christ's robe of righteousness. But another group doesn't know God, has no relationship or fellowship with Him, even though they know about the three angels and their messages. So among those people acquainted with the three angels, there exist those who know God, and those who don't.

But we find still another category of people. They *haven't* heard about the three angels. And you have the same two groups among them—those who know God, and those who don't.

Just before Jesus comes, polarization takes place. The lukewarm disappear, and everyone becomes either hot or cold. You've heard this old nursery rhyme: "There was a little girl, she had a little curl, right in the middle of her forehead; and when she was good, she was very, very good, and when she was bad, she was horrid." Before Jesus returns, those people who are good are going to become very, very good—but not in and of themselves. Those who are bad are going to be horrid. There will be no middle ground.

What causes the shaking—the polarization, the division—right on the borders of the Promised Land, the heavenly Canaan? The book *Early Writ-*

The Mighty Shaking

ings, in the chapter starting on page 269 (emphasis supplied), describes it: "I saw some, with strong faith and agonizing cries, pleading with God. Their countenances were pale and marked with deep anxiety, expressive of their internal struggle. Firmness and great earnestness was expressed in their countenances; large drops of perspiration fell from their foreheads."

If anyone has been going through a struggle and, because of the conflict, wondering if he had sufficient faith, he should take courage. Here we observe people with strong faith, yet they experience agonizing cries, pale countenances, deep anxiety, and internal struggle. That should give us courage. We must not think we're lost if we have anxiety. Evidently that's par for the course, especially at the end scene. But notice the next sentence: "*Now and then* their faces would light up with the marks of God's approbation, and again the same solemn, earnest, anxious look would settle upon them.

"Evil angels crowded around, pressing darkness upon them to shut out Jesus from their view [the evil angels have one purpose—to keep us from Jesus], that their eyes might be drawn to the darkness that surrounded them, and thus they be led to distrust God and murmur against Him. Their only safety was in keeping their eyes directed upward. . . .

"As the praying ones continued their earnest cries, *at times* a ray of light from Jesus came to them, to encourage their hearts and light up their countenances." Notice that God's encouragement came to them only occasionally.

Now another group is depicted. "Some, I saw, did not participate in this work of agonizing and pleading. They seemed indifferent and careless. They were not resisting the darkness around them, and it shut them in like a thick cloud. The angels of God left these and went to the aid of the earnest, praying ones." (We will notice also that the Holy Spirit leaves them and goes to the others.)

Now we come to the crucial point: "I asked the meaning of the shaking I had seen and was shown that it would be caused by the straight testimony called forth by the *counsel* of the True Witness to the Laodiceans." What was the counsel? It was the need for faith, love, Christ's righteousness, and the Holy Spirit—none other than the message of salvation through faith in Jesus Christ alone.

For a long time some people in our wilderness wandering have somehow gotten the idea that the straight testimony causing the shaking is the *rebuke* to Laodicea. Without question a rebuke will cause a shaking. If we wanted to have one, we could preach a burning sermon against meat eating and split the congregation right down the middle. All the meat eaters would stand on one side, and all the vegetarians on the other. And the next day the preacher would be run out of town.

Or we could begin really getting after the church members, reprimanding them for their lowered standards in terms of dress, adornment, or you name it. It's not that hard to get a shaking going.

The Mighty Shaking

But will that be what brings on the revival and the Holy Spirit? Many during our wilderness sojourn have had exactly that impression.

I remember a revival I heard about one time up in the Northwest. Based upon everyone's becoming a vegetarian, it went along OK until someone found a salmon in the deep freeze of the local elder, and that ended the matter.

Another group sought to bring on the great shaking and revival and reformation by getting members to take off their pins, watchbands, and tie clasps. As a young fellow, I listened carefully to some of their ideas, and I remember determining to take off my tie clasp and my watchband to help initiate the revival. But I got tired of having my tie go into the soup. So one day I got a bobby pin out of my wife's things and used it for a tie clasp. It worked fine. There were always plenty of bobby pins around, even in different colors.

But one day someone noticed my bobby pin and inquired, "What's that?"

"It's a bobby pin," I said.

"Why are you wearing a bobby pin?"

"Well, I don't believe in wearing tie clasps." Then I began to feel sort of proud of my bobby pin and discovered that the thing was ending up worse as far as my own experience was concerned than if I'd worn the tie clasp. One day it dawned on me that maybe I needed a little common sense, a little sanctified reason along with some of my endeavors. I got out my tie clasps again. Now if the *Lord* convicted me to leave off my tie clasp, I would do it. But I assure you that at that time I was doing it for the wrong reasons, and what it did to me proved it.

No, the shaking, final revival, and reformation that sweep the ranks of God's people before the crossing of the Jordan rest not upon the rebuke but upon the *counsel* of the True Witness to the Laodiceans. But how could people become perturbed when invited to seek faith and love and the Holy Spirit and Christ's righteousness? Isn't everyone in favor of that?

The only reason anyone would get upset would be if he had been depending upon something else for his salvation. Then it would be the same thing as pulling the rug out from underneath him. If I have been resting upon my good morality, behavior, and works—on all the things I do and don't do—for my certainty of salvation, and someone comes along and says, "That is not where it's at. Jesus alone is the basis of your salvation," I'm going to panic. Such people will resist and will try all kinds of maneuvers to oppose it, sometimes in subtle and pious ways. But that was true also in the days of Jesus. People always get shaken up when presented with the message of Christ and love and faith and total dependence upon God. Wherever Paul went, either a revival or a riot erupted. Any middle group soon disappeared.

"I asked the meaning of the shaking I had seen and was shown that it would be caused by the straight testimony called forth by the *counsel* of the True Witness to the Laodiceans. This will have its

The Mighty Shaking

effect upon the *heart* of the receiver." Now we're talking about something more than externals. "Some will not bear this straight testimony. They will rise up against it, and this is what will cause a shaking among God's people."

On the banks of the Jordan River you see all the people who know about the three angels shifting into two groups: those who know God and those who don't. Those who don't know God still keep up the works, but inside they are cold.

The interesting thing is that, during the shaking in the church, those outside the church who do not know about the three angels also polarize. They divide into the same two groups.

"Said the angel, 'List ye!' Soon I heard a voice like many musical instruments all sounding in perfect strains, sweet and harmonious. It surpassed any music I had ever heard, seeming to be full of mercy, compassion, and elevating, holy joy. It thrilled through my whole being. Said the angel, 'Look ye!' My attention was then turned to the company I had seen, who were mightily shaken. I was shown those whom I had before seen weeping and praying in agony of spirit. The company of guardian angels around them had been doubled, and they were clothed with an armor from their head to their feet. . . . They had obtained the victory, and it called forth from them the deepest gratitude and holy, sacred joy."

The issue in every temptation is to depend upon ourselves. When a person obtains the ultimate, final victory, by God's grace he has triumphed over self-dependence. That brings all other victories with it.

"The numbers of this company had lessened." Even among those who knew God, some had grown cold during the shaking and had lost their one-to-one contact with Him. The numbers lessen. "The careless and indifferent, who did not join with those who prized victory and salvation enough to perseveringly plead and agonize for it, did not obtain it, and they were left behind in darkness, and their places were immediately filled by others taking hold of the truth and coming into the ranks. Evil angels still pressed around them, but could have no power over them.

"I heard those clothed with the armor speak forth the truth with great power. It had effect. . . . I asked what had made this great change. An angel answered, 'It is the latter rain, the refreshing from the presence of the Lord, the loud cry of the third angel."

So just before Jesus comes, the world forms into two camps, a process represented by the terms "shaking" and "sifting,"—which come from an old method of threshing wheat. Farmers took the wheat out of the field, put it into a pan, and shook the pan. The wheat and chaff separated into two distinct parts. Then they tossed it up in the air, and if the wind was blowing, it would whisk away the chaff because it was light, and the wheat would fall back into the pan. The second process was known as the sifting. The wind separates the chaff out. So you have two parts: the shaking, with the chaff and

The Mighty Shaking

the wheat still in the pan—two distinct groups still in the church; and the sifting, when the chaff gets blown away.

Wind in Bible prophecy represents trouble, strife, and persecution. Even though two groups exist within the church, you don't find out who's who until trouble starts. The group that doesn't know God, can't take it. They leave.

I've heard people say, "The problem in our church and our country is that we don't have enough persecution. If we could just get some persecution going, why it would warm everybody up!" Trouble does not bring on the warming up, but rather the other way around.

As the angels leave the one group and double around the other, and the Holy Spirit does the same, the people clothed in the righteousness of Christ begin to take to others God's message with the power of the Holy Spirit and the latter rain. They carry the message about the three angels to those who know God but do not know about the three angels.

People who already possess an experience with God will easily see something in the truth that comes at that time. Accepting it, they'll fill the places of the lukewarm who left.

So at the end we will find only two groups. One comprises all the people who know God, some of which have just found out about the three angels. In the other group collect those who don't have a relationship with God. Among them are many who know about the three angels but never took the time to get to know God.

As a result of the latter rain, or outpouring of God's Spirit, the final movements that go like fire begin to take place. Soon Jesus appears in the clouds. Before He does, though, those people acquainted with final events but not God get panicky. They remember all the charts they have studied and see the events depicted on them happening in front of their eyes. Rushing over to God's people, they plead, "Help us. Tell us what to do. Quick! The smoke is beginning to rise for the last time. We need help." And no one will be able to do anything for them, because it's too late.

"The time of God's destructive judgments is the time of mercy for those who have no opportunity to learn what is true. Tenderly will the Lord look upon them. His heart of mercy is touched; his hand is still stretched out to save, while the door is closed to those who would not enter" (*Review and Herald*, July 5, 1906). There comes a time when people who have had all kinds of opportunities but have turned them down will discover it's too late to change their minds. For them the door has closed, while people who knew God but hadn't had the other opportunities will still be hearing the truth and accepting it.

I would like to suggest to you that this shaking is going on right now. It has been happening for some time and is getting more pronounced every day. It is the greatest sign of Jesus' soon return.

The only way anyone can cross the Jordan into the Promised Land is to rely upon Jesus' righteousness instead of his own.

The Mighty Shaking

A. T. Jones presented a talk in 1893 at a General Conference session. It was during the time when he and others clearly emphasized Christ as our only hope of salvation. "In that day there are going to be two parties there," he stated; "there are going to be some there when the door is shut, and they will want to go in, and they say, 'Lord, open unto us; we want to come in.'. . .

' "What have you done that you should go in? What right have you to enter the inheritance here? What claim have you upon that?'

' "Oh,' " they answer, ' " we are acquainted with you; we have eaten and drunk in thy presence. And thou hast taught in our streets. Yes, besides that, we have prophesied in thy name; in thy name we have cast out devils;. . . and have done many wonderful works. . . . Lord, is not that evidence enough? Open the door.' . . .

' "Depart from me, ye that work iniquity.' . . .

"There is going to be another company there that day—a great multitude that no man can number—all nations, and kindreds, and tongues, and people; and they will come up to enter in. . . . 'What have you done that you should enter here? What claim have you here?' . . .

' "I have not done anything at all to deserve it. I am a sinner, dependent only upon the grace of the Lord. Oh, I was so wretched, so completely a captive, and in such a bondage, that nobody could deliver me but the Lord himself; . . . so blind that no one but the Lord could cause me to see, so naked that no one could clothe me but the Lord himself.

All the claim that I have is what Jesus has done for me. . . . When in my wretchedness I cried, he delivered me; when in my misery I needed comfort, he comforted me all the way; when in my poverty I begged, he gave me riches; when in my blindness I asked him to show me the way, that I might know the way, he led all the way, and made me to see; when I was so naked that no one could clothe me, why, he gave me this garment that I have on; so all that I can present, all that I have to present, as that upon which I can enter, any claim that would cause me to enter, is just what he has done for me; if that will not pass me, then I am left out; and that will be just, too. If I am left out, I have no complaint to make. But, oh, will this not entitle me to enter and possess the inheritance?' . . .

And the heavenly witness answers and says, ' "Why, yes. We are perfectly satisfied with him. . . . The deliverance that you obtained from his wretchedness is that which our Lord wrought. . . . That garment that he has on, the Lord gave it to him—the Lord wove it and it is all divine. It is only Christ. Why, *yes. He can come in.*' . . .

"And then, brethren, there will come over the gates a voice of sweetest music, full of the gentleness and compassion for my Saviour—the voice will come from within, 'Come in, thou blessed of the Lord. . . . Why standest thou without?' And the gate will be swung wide open, and we shall have 'an abundant entrance into the everlasting kingdom of our Lord and Saviour, Jesus Christ.' "

Someone spontaneously began singing, "Jesus

paid it all." And the audience took up the song: "All to him I owe. Sin had left a crimson stain. He washed it white as snow."

Chapter 13

Crossing the Jordan

The name *Joshua* for a long time created in my mind the picture of a man clad with armor up to his teeth, wearing helmet, shield, and sword—a big sword, ready to lop off the head of the closest enemy. I thought of a man who was a warrior, ready to do battle at the drop of a hat. But that really is not Joshua. In a sense, he was a type of Jesus.

The people of Israel camped by the Jordan River, across from Canaan. Finally they were about to enter it after years of wilderness wandering. Moses was dead. But just before he died, he had a vision of the land of Canaan and the Promised Land. And before his death he wrote down all the instruction necessary to take the people through.

In the modern Advent movement we also had someone who died on the borders of the heavenly Canaan, who saw a vision of the Promised Land, and who wrote down all the instruction necessary to see the Advent people through.

We will skip ahead in events, returning for a final look at Moses in Chapter 15. As we study the history of the people of Israel in the time immedi-

Crossing the Jordan

ately prior to and immediately following the crossing of Jordan, we will find lessons, particularly for the individual spiritual life, that are worth noting.

Before the counterpart of Moses died, she penned, "We have nothing to fear for the future, except as we shall forget the way the Lord has led us" (*Testimonies to Ministers*, p. 31). Often we have used that phrase to pat ourselves on the back, to congratulate ourselves on our growth and statistical accomplishments. But we shouldn't still be here, and we have nothing to be proud of. God's work should have been finished by someone a long time ago. So we need to read the statement differently. "We have nothing to fear for the future, except as we forget that *the Lord has stayed with us* in spite of us and our past history." Scripture says that John was the disciple whom Jesus loved, but the tense of the word in the Greek means that he was the disciple that Jesus *kept on loving*—in spite of his shortcomings. So let's not congratulate ourselves and feel that we have achieved. We have not. Organized religion, including our own, has failed. It's about time we begin to face that fact more frequently and more realistically.

We know that God finally took the ancient people into the land of Canaan, not because they were worthy, but because the nations of the Canaanites had filled up their cup of corruption, and God saw no point in waiting longer. How many times have we prayed, "And Lord, when at last Thou comest in thy kingdom, grant that we might be worthy to have an abundant entrance . . ." We will never be worthy. The only reason anyone will ever enter God's kingdom is because Jesus is worthy, not us.

Joshua was one of the two adults who left Egypt and finally entered the Promised Land. The other was Caleb. Even Moses, Aaron, and Miriam had died in the wilderness. Evidently Joshua, Moses' prime minister, associated closely with him. He had been on the top of Mount Sinai with Moses when the Hebrew leader had communicated with God. Early in the trek from Egypt to Canaan, Joshua had participated in the defeat of the Amalekites at Rephidim before the Exodus people had reached Sinai. He was also one of the twelve spies that went from Kadesh-barnea and came back with the good report—one of the two who said that the people of Israel could possess the land and who almost got stoned for it. In spite of being sent back for forty years of exile in the desert after that experience, he remained true to God. We are told that Joshua was a man who spent much time in meditation and prayer.

Joshua was the man who commanded the sun and moon to stand still and they obeyed, and yet Joshua failed on occasion. After the victory at Jericho, the people of Israel had the impression that *they* had conquered the city. When they saw the little village of Ai, the next city on the map, they never even consulted God about it. They went ahead on their own, tried to overpower Ai with just a handful of soldiers, and came back bruised and bleeding. Joshua went from total trust in God to trusting in himself again—after he had crossed the Jordan!

Joshua was a meek, unselfish man, When Israel finally began to divide the territory of Canaan among the different tribes, he only asked for one city. And although many think of him chiefly as a warrior, he was also known as a man of God. One of the greatest testimonies that we have about Joshua occurs at the close of his life when he stood before the people and made his call for decision: "Choose you this day whom ye will serve." Notice he didn't ask them to decide what they were going to *do*—rather, *whom* they were going to serve. This is the essence of all of the experiences of genuine faith. And Scripture records that as a result of his appeal the people followed the Lord all his days, and all the days of the elders that outlived him. His life offers a classic example of one who had chosen to become a servant of God.

Patriarchs and Prophets, page 509, speaks of the day when the sun and the moon stood still. Joshua received the promise that God would overthrow Israel's enemies, "yet he put forth as earnest effort as though success depended upon the armies of Israel alone. He did all that human energy could do, and then he cried in faith for divine aid. The secret of success is the union of divine power with human effort." I have had people quote this to me again and again when we talk about absolute dependence upon God, letting God do it. But they always fail to quote the rest of the paragraph: "Those who achieve the greatest results are those who rely most implicitly upon the Almighty Arm. The man who commanded, 'Sun, stand thou still upon Gibeon; and thou, Moon, in the valley of Ajalon,' is the man who for hours lay prostrate upon the earth in prayer in the camp at Gilgal. The men of prayer are the men of power."

We have never taken the position that surrender to God leaves us effortless. But we do claim that the one who lets God control him does whatever God leads him to do naturally. The trusting Christian life involves a great deal of effort, but it is natural, not forced. The planned, deliberate effort is in going down on your face, in your tent in your camp at Gilgal, spending time with God. Joshua did, and God selected him as the one to take Moses' place and lead the people across the Jordan River into the Promised Land.

"Now after the death of Moses the servant of the Lord it came to pass, that the Lord spake unto Joshua the son of Nun, Moses' minister, saying, Moses my servant is dead; now therefore arise, go over this Jordan, thou, and all this people, unto the land which I do give to them, even to the children of Israel." "Have not I commanded thee? Be strong and of good courage; be not afraid, neither be thou dismayed: for the Lord thy God is with thee whithersoever thou goest. Then Joshua commanded the officers of the people, saying, Pass through the host, and command the people, saying, Prepare you victuals; for within three days ye shall pass over this Jordan, to go in to possess the land, which the Lord your God giveth you to pos-

Crossing the Jordan

sess it" (Joshua 1:1, 2, 9-11). Get a sack lunch ready. We are going to brown bag it the next few days as we cross the Jordan River.

In verses 16-18, notice how the people responded. "And they answered Joshua, saying, All that thou commandest us we will do, and whithersoever thou sendest us, we will go. According as we hearkened unto Moses in all things [which may not have been as much of an encouragement to Joshua as the people intended] so will we hearken unto thee: only the Lord thy God be with thee, as he was with Moses. Whosoever he be that doth rebel against thy commandment, and will not hearken unto thy words in all that thou commandest him, he shall be put to death: only be strong and of a good courage." It was a response with teeth in it. But we have no evidence that they had to put anyone to death.

And the Lord said to Joshua, "Thou shalt command the priests that bear the ark of the covenant, saying, When ye are come to the brink of the water of Jordan, ye shall stand still in Jordan. And Joshua said unto the children of Israel, Come hither, and hear the words of the Lord your God. And Joshua said, Hereby ye shall know that the living God is among you. . . . Behold, the ark of the covenant of the Lord of all the earth passeth over before you into Jordan " "And as they that bare the ark were come unto Jordan, and the feet of the priests that bare the ark were dipped in the brim of the water, (for Jordan overfloweth all his banks all the time of the harvest,) that the waters which came down from above stood and rose up upon an heap. . . . and the priests that bare the ark of the covenant of the Lord stood firm on dry ground in the midst of Jordan, and all the Israelites passed over on dry ground, until all the people were passed clean over Jordan" (Joshua 3:8-11, 15-17).

Perhaps some have seen the Jordan. I remember being a bit disappointed, when we were there several years ago, watching a baptism near the place where John the Baptist had baptized. The river wasn't that big. It was deep in spots and shallow elsewhere. At places during the regular season of the year one could wade across at fords. But the children of Israel passed through it during floodtime, and I understand the river can get rather turbulent and high. But whether it was a small river or a big one is beside the point. Whether God divides a small or big river, it's still a miracle— enough of a miracle that the inhabitants of Canaan didn't try to rationalize it. They had heard about the Red Sea years before and hadn't forgotten. The people feared and quaked.

For a long time we have tended to interpret this kind of story as a sample of how to exercise faith. We have gotten the impression that the reason the waters opened was because the people put their feet in.

Did the water at the Jordan open up because the feet touched the water? Or did the feet touch the water because they knew the water would open up?

Human pride wants to hold onto the idea that we can do something to make it happen. "Please,

God, let me have some part in it, so that I (but we don't say it out loud) can have a little credit for its happening."

When the devil fails to get people to work on their works, to try to get to heaven by their own achievements, then he seeks to lead them to work on their faith. But faith is not something you work on. Faith is spontaneous and comes from knowing God.

But even in the case of the Jordan River, the *people's* feet didn't touch the water before it opened. They were far behind the priests with the ark. If you want to take the lesson all the way through, then no one should do anything until he sees the minister do it. And we're told that's not right. We are not supposed to depend on anybody, including the minister.

I would like to invite you to turn loose from the old idea that it happens because you put your feet in the water. We have held it too long. Genuine faith results in absolute dependence upon God, even though the evidence is "not seen" (Hebrews 11:1).

What does the crossing of the Jordan have to say to the modern Advent people? You will find a clue in 1 Corinthians 10: 1, 2: "Moreover, brethren, I would not that ye should be ignorant, how that all our fathers were under the cloud, and all passed through the sea: and were all *baptized* unto Moses in the cloud and in the sea." Paul interprets the Red Sea crossing as a baptism. But we have evidence that not everyone who went through the Red Sea had been converted. A "mixed multitude" accompanied them, and I suppose we don't have to argue the point that not everyone baptized into the Advent movement has been converted. The devil has seen to that. We also recognize traits remaining from Egyptian life-style.

If we were to transfer the Red Sea experience to the individual life, we could apply it to our initial baptism when we accept deliverance and head toward the Promised Land. Have you ever had the experience of going through a long, desolate wilderness even after you first became a Christian? Some people have thought that conversion and baptism were supposed to complete the whole work. But we must remember that it is only the beginning. Many have become disenchanted and discouraged because they thought that conversion and baptism would end all problems and failures. Many failures and problems occurred among the people of God after the baptism at the Red Sea. In the Exodus movement, most of them died before they entered the Promised Land, and the same is true in the Advent movement.

But notice something else here. If the baptism was the Red Sea experience, then going through the Jordan River at the close of the wilderness wandering would also be another symbolic baptism. Some people would choose to call it the baptism of the Holy Spirit. Taylor Bunch termed it the latter rain, as opposed to the Red Sea experience being the early rain. One thing we do know about the latter rain is that it is the endowment of the Holy

Spirit upon a corporate body of people. It is the same outpouring of the Holy Spirit upon a group that was available to individuals prior to that time.

The Holy Spirit works progressively in the Christian's life. And the Spirit operates in a similar manner in the life of a corporate group. The first activity of the Holy Spirit is to convict the sinner, the second to convert him. And that is where we often think He stops—after the Red Sea, wandering in the wilderness. But He must also cleanse the Christian. His final work is to commission for service. The fruits of the Holy Spirit come under the third phase, and the gifts of the Spirit under the fourth. When a group of people have allowed the Holy Spirit to cleanse them and to commission them for service, the world will witness a great outpouring of the Holy Spirit, called the latter rain. The baptism at the Jordan River would represent the baptism of the Holy Spirit, the empowering for service.

The people who crossed the Jordan River into Canaan had not let themselves be shaken out in the wilderness. Evidently they had at least a minimum of faith. God wasn't taking them into the Promised Land because they were worthy, but He had shaken out the ones who had proven themselves definitely unworthy. He had a group of people who would cross the Jordan River at His command. They would willingly perform a seemingly ridiculous thing like walk around Jericho for seven days—seven times on the seventh day—and do nothing but blow trumpets. It takes at least a minimum of faith to do that. Yet they would still take over the reins and not depend upon God to conquer Ai. So evidently during and after the latter rain we still will be learning the lessons of trust.

Exciting things have happened at the Jordan River through the years. Elijah struck the waters with his mantel, and they parted. Elisha returned to the Jordan after Elijah's ascension and did the same thing. Naaman bathed in the Jordan at the instruction of Elisha, and God healed him of his leprosy. John the Baptist baptized hundreds of people in its waters. Jesus Himself was baptized there at the beginning of His public ministry.

When we talk about the troubled waters of the Jordan at flood tide we allude to something that will also take place at the end of time, before Jesus comes again. When God pours out the latter rain, the one group of people who have come unto total, absolute surrender and control by God will encounter persecution. The shaking will have separated everyone into one of two sides. As the Holy Spirit leaves the unrighteous, the flood of fury, wickedness, murder, and hatred will be incomprehensible.

The Bible says it will be "a time of trouble, such as never was" (Daniel 12:1). We are told that it will require a faith that many of us "do not now possess" and have been "too indolent to obtain" (*The Great Controversy*, p. 622). Some of us are sitting around waiting for it to hit us someday, hoping that the Holy Spirit will do for us what He did with the neighbor next door. We are too lazy to seek God

Crossing the Jordan

for ourselves. But the meaningful Christian life does put forth some deliberate, legitimate effort. It is the effort to seek a relationship with God.

We are also warned that the time of trouble will be of such a nature that it will be worse in reality than in anticipation (*ibid.*) Usually it is the other way around. You have an appointment at the dentist's office, you fret and stew and pull your hair out before you go, and when you get there you find out that it wasn't nearly as bad as you had thought it would be. We used to climb up on the roof of the garage when we were kids. Someone would push the ladder away, and then we would wait to see who would jump first. I can remember going through a terrible struggle there on the garage roof. The longer I waited, the worse it got. Finally, when I got up enough courage to leap off, I found out it wasn't nearly as bad as I had thought.

In the times just around the corner, it's just the opposite. The trouble will be far worse than we can imagine. The murky floodwaters of the Jordan represent trouble.

"If thou hast run with the footmen, and they have wearied thee, then how canst thou contend with horses? and if in the land of peace, wherein thou trustedst, they wearied thee, then how wilt thou do in the swelling of Jordan?" (Jeremiah 12:5). Perhaps we think that although we have difficulties with the little things now, when the big times come we will rise to the occasion. Then we will step forward and say, "I will be true. You can burn me, but I won't falter." But the results of the tests in little things that come each day demonstrate to us how we will face the big ones. We think we will be able to brave the high seas, but we drown in the bathtub. Or we dream of skydiving, but we're scared to jump off the back porch. Jeremiah asked that if you can't make it with the footmen, how are you going to be able to run with horses?

If you would like to know exactly how you will react when the "swelling of Jordan" comes, take a look at how you face the little crises of today. That is how you will respond then. It is a challenge not to look at ourselves and our failures, but to look to God, and to depend upon Him, as Joshua did, realizing that He is sufficient even though we aren't.

Chapter 14

Jericho to Ai

In a sense, even though you have arrived in the Promised Land, the battle isn't over yet—contrary to what we would ordinarily think in our comparison between the Exodus and Advent movements. We have suggested that crossing the Jordan into the Promised Land would correspond to the finishing of God's work on earth and the coming of Jesus. As far as the comparison between the two movements goes, probably so. But you can personally enter the spiritual Promised Land by faith and still waver. We will notice in this chapter the individual lessons we need to learn rather than the comparison between the two movements.

"And it came to pass, when Joshua was by Jericho, that he lifted up his eyes and looked, and, behold, there stood a man over against him with his sword drawn in his hand: and Joshua went unto him, and said unto him, Art thou for us, or for our adversaries? And he said, Nay; but as captain of the host of the Lord am I now come. And Joshua fell on his face to the earth, and did worship, and said unto him, What saith my lord unto his servant?

And the captain of the Lord's host said unto Joshua, Loose thy shoe from off thy foot; for the place whereon thou standest is holy. And Joshua did so" (Joshua 5:13-15).

Jericho was one of the most formidable fortresses in the land of Canaan. Joshua did not venture to move without seeking God's direction at every step. The story indicates that Joshua had left the camp, had gone to a quiet place to meditate and pray and seek to learn the Lord's will. We believe that it was Jesus Christ Himself who came to Joshua, although Scripture doesn't call Him by that name.

"Now Jericho was straitly shut up because of the children of Israel: none went out, and none came in. And the Lord said unto Joshua, See, I have given into thine hand Jericho, and the king thereof, and the mighty men of valour" (Joshua 6:1, 2). Jericho was in the Promised Land, and the Promised Land was a gift. God never intended for Israel to conquer the territory through warfare, but by strict obedience to His directions. Here we have in the story of the fall of Jericho a classic example of someone's following God's directions.

The Lord directed Joshua, and he in turn led the people. They followed the directions given. God had wanted to give them Jericho and the entire Promised Land forty years before, but He couldn't. For four decades we have seen the ebb and flow, the changing tide of faith. Scripture portrays people struggling, living, suffering, dying, all trying to learn the one lesson—the lesson of Jericho

Jericho to Ai

and Ai—of self-distrust and of total dependence upon God.

But did you know that if you are a follower of Jesus Christ, if you have a personal relationship with Him, that you are already in the Promised Land, that you are experiencing heaven? "As through Jesus we enter into rest, heaven begins here.... In thus coming [to Christ] we begin the life eternal. Heaven is a ceaseless approaching to God through Christ" (*The Desire of Ages*, p. 331).

If you know what it means to come to God each day through prayer and study of His Word, then heaven has already begun for you. But that doesn't mean that the conflict has ceased. Jesus' battle is over. He won His conflict at the cross, and in a sense we have triumphed through Jesus and His merits. But Jesus has plans for His people that have included being more than conquerors through Him who loved us. Our victory in the heaven that begins here continues only as long as we, on a daily basis, accept the victory Jesus obtained for us. The battle to continue to claim it is an ongoing struggle.

Notice that as the Hebrews entered the Promised Land, the battle did not end for them. They had entered Canaan but had not subdued it. To human appearances, as they looked at the walled cities and the fortresses that seemed to reach up to the skies, the struggle to gain possession of the land would apparently be long and difficult. We can learn from Israel for our individual experiences today.

First of all, notice that Joshua went to his knees

before Jesus and triumphed over Jericho before the battle ever took place. So it is in the Christian life. Every victory over every temptation that we really gain we always achieve before the temptation comes. We do not overcome temptations at the time we meet them. Rather, we master them beforehand, or not at all, Never can we encounter the enemy on the spur of the moment and experience God's power over him. God's power is to be known long before. If we have not surrendered to Jesus at the time the devil appears with all of his subtle ways, we have little chance of doing it then. The best I can do is fail and repent and come to Him again. And of course that is possible. But the Jericho way is the one God intends for every individual.

Joshua received instructions about what to do with Jericho. But they sound absurd to human reasoning. Can you imagine a group of soldiers walking around a city? Imagine the frustration they would have gone through. The struggle was not to fight the enemy, but to *not* fight the enemy. No army marching around Jericho once a day could escape the terrible inner conflict of wanting to whip out their bows and arrows and at least pick off a few guards from the top of the wall. It would make the attack easier later. But no, all they could do was walk around the city and meditate. They couldn't even talk:

"And Joshua had commanded the people, saying, Ye shall not shout, nor make any noise with your voice, neither shall any word proceed out of

Jericho to Ai

your mouth" (Joshua 6:10). In a sense you see a group of people going around Jericho for their morning devotions day after day, for six days. Finally the seventh day arrives and around they go, seven times. "Then the lamb ram sheep horns began to blow, the trumpets began to sound. Joshua commanded the people to shout, and the walls came tumbling down."

One of our nation's military experts at a military academy one day gave a sample from the Bible to his class. He made quite a speech about Joshua's clever manuevers at Jericho. Joshua was really smart, the man said. He used psychological warfare. Let's not deny the fact that the experience must have psyched out the people. If we had been in Jericho, we would probably have reacted the same way too. But then the military expert proceeded to show that Joshua used a natural means to get the walls to tumble down. He had the people blow the trumpets, and they probably had them tuned to the right note. Like Giovanni Matinelli, the Italian singer who supposedly could break a glass by finding the proper vibration, Joshua knew the right frequency that would cause the rocks to crumble. You could go through all kinds of explanations, but we know that the armies of heaven overthrew Jericho, and we accept that fact by faith.

The angels toppled the walls, and evidently it wasn't too hard for them, either. Man's part was simply to obey God's instructions. Part of them stipulated that they must make no assault on the city. They were not to attack. All they did was shout and give God the glory. "The Israelites had not gained the victory by their own power; the conquest had been wholly the Lord's.... It was to be impressed upon Israel that in the conquest of Canaan they were not to fight for themselves, but simply as instruments to execute the will of God" (*Patriarchs and Prophets*, p. 491).

An instrument, a passive thing, is something that the artisan or soldier or farmer uses. The ax is effective because of the one who uses it. The painter's brush accomplishes something because of the painter. It doesn't mean that nothing happens. Plenty does, but we are simply the tools of God's power and might. The people who surrounded Jericho were not inactive. We find nothing of quietism here. But the effort they put forth had its motivation in faith in God and His work through them. We are told that in the conquest of Jericho God wanted people to become accustomed to relying wholly upon their Divine Leader (*ibid.*, p. 493). Have you learned that lesson yet? When you first became a Christian did you discover that you could look to God, could depend upon His power and His strength? But have you gradually faded away from that?

How easy it is, even though we don't want to, to begin trusting our own strength, even immediately after knowing the presence and power of God. This is precisely the story of Jericho and Ai.

Ai was a little town on the other side of Jericho. It had only about twelve thousand people. Joshua sent a couple of spies to look it over. They came back and reported, "All we need are a few thousand men." Dispatching two or three thousand men, Joshua didn't spend time off by himself away from the camp, seeking the Lord's plan and strength.

"The great victory that God had gained for them had made the Israelites self-confident. Because He had promised them the land of Canaan they felt secure, and failed to realize that divine help alone could give them success. Even Joshua laid his plans for the conquest of Ai without seeking counsel from God" (*ibid.*, p. 493). Most of us cannot be trusted with power. It would destroy us. Joshua, one of the greatest men who ever lived, who could take over after Moses, failed the test, though he had gone through the experiences at Jordan and Jericho. The "I did it" problem trips us all up.

The two or three thousand men made an assault on the city, something that God never intended. All of a sudden the inhabitants of Ai came rushing out of the city, and God's people hightailed it down the hill, through the ravines, like scared rabbits. Thirty-six men died.

Joshua, a warrior, could have said, "We didn't make the right plans. Let's get more men, use different strategy." But instead, according to Scripture, Joshua "fell to the earth upon his face" before the Lord. Realizing his problem, he admitted that he had been depending upon his own strength.

But another interesting aspect enters the story. Three verses, right in the middle of Joshua 6, speak of "the accursed thing." After the conquest of Jericho, God did not intend for the people to take anything for themselves from the city. He said, "And the city shall be accursed, even it, and all that are therein." The margin of your Bible helps you a little with the original meaning: the city shall be *devoted*. Everything that was in it, as a result of God's victory, was devoted to God. No man was to take any of the results of the Lord's triumph. But we know of one who took something.

Achan had been through the Jordan River. He had seen the waters piled up and Jericho fall. Despite having witnessed the mighty power of God, he still coveted and stole silver and gold and a fashionable mantle from Shinar. It was one reason why the whole congregation suffered, though not the only one. I remember having the impression that the reason that Ai defeated Israel was because of Achan. Actually Israel's failure at Ai was because Joshua, the soldiers, and the leaders depended upon themselves. In a spiritual sense, Joshua had taken of "the accursed thing" himself. You don't have to take silver and gold and garments from God in order to steal from Him. All you have to do is to claim a little glory and credit to yourself for God's success.

Suppose we have some great victory in the cause of God. We lead one thousand souls to Christ in some large city. Now if that were to happen, I am quite sure we would all know theoretically that the Holy Spirit was responsible. But who do you suppose would be tempted to send his picture in to the *Adventist Review* along with the photograph of the thousand (to make sure everyone knew about it).

I don't think we should blame Achan for the whole problem of Ai. But Achan was different from Joshua. When Joshua realized the problem, that he had been depending upon himself, he bowed in repentance and cried out to God. Achan, when he saw what the problem was, kept silent.

God gave instructions, and the people began to cast lots. Achan realized that the armies had come back defeated. Then he saw the grief of Joshua and heard that someone had committed a terrible crime in the camp of Israel. He even heard the specific nature of the crime, and got tight stomach muscles right there. The lots pointed to Achan's tribe. They cast lots again, and it chose Achan's family. Once more, and the lot fell on his own household, his own tent. But he still stood there in absolute silence. His problem was one of pure rebellion. He had no sorrow over his defiance of God, and that's the difference between the righteous and the wicked. Righteous people sometimes do wicked things, but they know how to fall on their faces in sorrow and repentance. Wicked people do wicked things, and they thrust out their chins at God and cast their contempt in His face.

Finally, when the lot indicated Achan, Joshua asked him to confess, and only then did he do so. But what did he say? "I saw the gold and the silver and I saw this goodly Babylonish garment." If I had been in Achan's shoes, I don't think I would have called it "goodly" by about that time. I would have considered it as quite ugly. Someday there will be people who confess that Jesus is Lord, but it will be too late, because the confession is wrung from them by the circumstances of the moment, not by any deep, heartfelt love or repentance.

Israel took Achan, with everything he possessed, including his family and children, and stoned and burned them, then heaped a pile of rocks over them.

"Have you considered why it was that all who were connected with Achan were also subjects of the punishment of God? It was because they had not been trained and educated according to the directions given them in the great standard of the law of God. Achan's parents had educated their son in such a way that he felt free to disobey the word of the Lord. The principles inculcated in his life led him to deal with his children in such a way that they also were corrupted. Mind acts and reacts upon the mind, and the punishment, which included the relations of Achan with himself, reveals the fact that all were involved in the transgression" (*Child Guidance*, p. 234).

The record of God's dealings with those of Israel who had crossed the Jordan after so many years and yet who still took credit to themselves and fell at Ai demonstrates His love. Even Joshua trusted God at one point, then himself at the next. And here today we are still trying to learn the same lesson: to depend upon God, to let Him do His mighty works, and us not to take credit. Although we are slow to grasp it, God is extremely patient with us.

"There are those who have known the pardoning love of Christ and who really desire to be children of God, yet they realize that their character is imperfect, their life faulty, and they are ready to doubt whether their hearts have been renewed by the Holy Spirit. To such I would say, Do not draw back in despair. We shall often have to bow down and weep at the feet of Jesus because of our shortcomings and mistakes; but we are not to be discouraged. Even if we are overcome by the enemy, we are not cast off, not forsaken and rejected of God. No; Christ is at the right hand of God, who also maketh intercession for us. . . . If you will but yield yourself to Him, He that hath begun a good work in you will carry it forward to the day of Jesus Christ. Pray more fervently; believe more fully. As we come to distrust our own power, let us trust the power of our Redeemer, and we shall praise Him who is the health of our countenance" (*Steps to Christ*, p. 64). Are you having a hard time learning to distrust your own power and to really trust God's? So did Israel; so did Joshua. Does that mean that we should fold up our tents and give up? No.

Some will wonder what to do about the Achans in the camp. The zealot exclaims, "That's our trouble! That's the problem with the church today, the reason God's work isn't finished." I know half a dozen myself, know what they are doing. Perhaps we ought to have a board meeting and put them out of the church. Then we can have God's blessings. But notice this statement: "When the church is in difficulty, when coldness and spiritual declension exist, giving occasion for the enemies of God to triumph, then, instead of folding their hands and lamenting their unhappy state, let its members inquire if there is not an Achan in the camp." That sounds like good ammunition. Let's get rid of all the Achans. But don't forget the next sentence: "With humiliation and searching of heart, let each seek to discover the hidden sins that shut out God's presence" (*Patriarchs and Prophets*, p. 497). Who are the Achans we are advised to look for? *We* are. We don't go on a witch-hunt but look in the mirror.

Yet all the time God is patient. Scripture sketches the history of Israel from the time of the Jordan and Jericho down to the end of their probation. We find great people like Gideon, who trust God, and even ones like Samson, one of the big mysteries of the Bible, who did some of his terrible deeds through the power of God. It seems that God would not have stayed around long enough to let people misuse Him. David trusted totally in God early in the game, but later on he fell into great sin. Elijah stood on the top of Mount Carmel, faced all the prophets of Baal, called fire down from heaven, and won a great victory for God that day. Then he had to pray seven times for rain, because he had gotten self-confident at Carmel, and God couldn't answer his prayer immediately because Elijah would have taken the credit for it. The next day he fled from Jezebel. Then there is King Jehoshaphat, who showed what can happen when a whole army depends upon God. But they are only examples.

Chapter 15

The Song of Moses and the Lamb*

"And Moses went up from the plains of Moab unto the mountain of Nebo, to the top of Pisgah, that is over against Jericho. And the Lord shewed him all the land of Gilead, unto Dan. And all Naphtali, and the land of Ephraim, and Manasseh, and all the land of Judah, unto the utmost sea. And the south, and plain of the valley of Jericho, the city of palm trees, unto Zoar. And the Lord said unto him, This is the land which I sware unto Abraham, unto Isaac, and unto Jacob, saying, I will give it unto thy seed: I have caused thee to see it with thine eyes, but thou shalt not go over thither. So Moses the servant of the Lord died there in the land of Moab, according to the word of the Lord. And he buried him in a valley in the land of Moab, over against

---

*Charles T. Everson preached this sermon at a General Conference in the 1930s. I learned about it from those who remembered hearing it. Later I obtained permission from his widow to look for it in his files. To my thrill I found his notes verbatim. To my knowledge, the sermon was never printed. I have chosen to include with it excerpts from the chapter "The Death of Moses," in *Patriarchs and Prophets,* pages 470-477, and the poem on the death of Moses by Cecil Frances Alexander (1818-1895).

Beth-peor: but no man knoweth of his sepulchre unto this day" (Deuteronomy 34:1-6).

The two great characters for the last days are Moses and Elijah. Moses, one of the leading prophets of all time, represents those who die and will be resurrected at Christ's second coming. Something about the song of Moses especially applies to God's people. The Bible says we will sing the song of Moses and the Lamb. Moses, the man who talked to God face-to-face, would never have entered history except for his mother, Jochebed.

"Pharaoh charged all his people, saying, Every son that is born ye shall cast into the river" (Exodus 1:22). When the decree was in full force, Moses was born. His mother kept him hid for three months at home and finally placed him in a basket floating on the bosom of the Nile. Pharaoh's daughter was the offspring of the child's greatest enemy, but God gave her a mother's love. It was love at first sight.

Moses' mother lived near the palace in a little house provided for her. She became a servant to her son, to win him for God. Near the Egyptian palace, with its black arts, witchcraft, spiritism of the deepest dye—without a preacher, without a Sabbath School, without a young people's society, without a church school—a lone woman, in the midnight darkness of Egypt, prayed and wept. Through her tears she taught him of the things of heaven so well that the dazzling splendor of Egypt could not attract him.

The throne, the greatest seat of authority and power in the world of his day, beckoned him. On the other hand there stood a band of slaves that his mother had told him were his people. She took him out and showed him the Israelites, dressed only in their loincloths, with bandanna handkerchiefs around their heads, digging with their bare hands in the clay pits, their brown backs all cut up by the taskmaster's lash. A smell of garlic and onions lingered about them. Moses' mother told him, "These, my son, are your people."

"It can't be possible," he exclaimed. They were such a low stratum of humanity. But she had taught him so well that he chose that band of clay-digging slaves as his future companions for life. Rather than accepting the throne of Egypt with the greatest cultural minds of ancient times, he decided to suffer affliction with the people of God. He knew what the choice meant.

When your boy or girl comes to the great decision, and the world offers them position, pleasure, honor, if only they will give up their faith, what weighs most with them? Do God's people look small, insignificant, without a future? Remember that while we might not be a great people, Moses had but a downtrodden, clay-digging band of slaves to choose as his. And he joined them with all his heart. He loved them to the end and was never sorry that he made the decision.

A man with a high brow and intellectual face sits in the wilderness with a few paltry sheep around him. He looks strangely out of place, tending a few sheep that a lad could shepherd for pennies a day. Why was this great intellect holding a shepherd boy's job? Because he was not ready for his great task. He was a quick-tempered man, who could whip out a dagger and stick it into a man's back and then bury his body in the sand. It took him forty years in the wilderness to learn his lesson—a long, desolate experience. Forty years, while the people of God cried for deliverance from the taskmaster's lash. But they must wait until Moses was ready. The sheep taught him, and when the forty years ended, God said of him, "He is the meekest man in all the earth."

Perhaps it seemed to you that your days were being irretrievably lost in your wilderness experience. But God has always been there, waiting in the burning bush to call you as soon as you have learned your lesson. And it did not take long, once Moses was ready to deliver Israel.

After his great sacrifice, the people gave no response, no word of appreciation. People for whom he had forsaken everything responded with nothing but murmuring, backbiting, and faultfinding. He never could please them. They accused him of bringing them into the desert to let them die of thirst. When they became thirsty and their children cried for water, the great rabble arose like a storm cloud. He was alone. What could he do against ignorant, maddened slaves looking for stones to crush his skull? All he could do was flee to God for protection. No wonder Scripture says he talked to God like a man speaks to his friend.

He would tell God that he must have water or they would soon hurl rocks at him. God said, "I will

The Song of Moses and the Lamb

bring water out of the rock." And the people calmed down.

Then they milled around because they couldn't sow and reap in the sands of the desert. God rained down bread from heaven. But they complained about the manna that the angels eat and wished themselves back in Egypt with the garlic and onions. Their highest ideal seemed to be garlic and onions and Baal and licentiousness. Moses heard nothing from the people he had rescued from the hardest bondage but complaints, murmurings, and threats to kill him "Not a thank you," says Moses, "have I heard from their lips." He came in among the congregation and thought to find a company of angels ready for translation.

We have expected great appreciation for the sacrifice we made to take up the faith and were heartbroken when we found ourselves criticized, backbitten, with no end of faultfinding and apparent lack of sympathy. Disappointed, perhaps we exclaimed, "Is it possible that this is really God's people? Why, the world appreciates me more than they do!" Don't forget the song of Moses and the Lamb.

Moses was not only not appreciated and continually found fault with, but his life was in peril again and again. When tempted to leave the people of God, I wish you would keep something in mind. The people of Israel finally sank so low and became so rebellious and licentious and faultfinding that apparently God became discouraged with them, and said, "I will end this travesty on religion. I will sweep these ungrateful wretches off the earth. I will destroy all, including Aaron." The Lord said to Moses, "Let me alone . . . that I may consume them: and I will make of thee a great nation."

Moses might have thought, "You're right. You can't make anything of these lowbrows, this garlic-loving, uncultured mob. With me as the beginning of a new people, You are going to get somewhere. I have culture, education, and everything You need to found a real nation upon."

Some people leave the faith because they lose a job in the church. Suppose God gave the leaders of this kind of people such an offer. Wouldn't they jump at it? But they will never sing the song of Moses and the lamb.

Moses was not thinking of himself, his fame, or his honor. He had given up everything for God years before. Long before, he had united his heart and soul to his people, had learned to love them because they were God's people. Now he would not give them up. His love for them was like God's love for unworthy man. Immediately he began to intercede for them, reminding God of His love for them and how he could not bear to be separated from them. Over and over he repeated it, but his case was desperate. God's decision to destroy the Hebrews seemed apparently irrevocable. But Moses held on, pleading. He placed before God every reason he could find for urging Him to save them. And yet they were a people who again and again were ready to take up rocks at a moment's notice and stone him, leaving his body rotting in

The Song of Moses and the Lamb

the wilderness for the vultures to devour.

Are you prepared to sing the song of Moses and the Lamb? Moses loved a people a hundred times more unlovable than those we see today. But he would not give them up for all the world. Do you admire Moses' love for God's people? Or do you allow some small insult to drive you away from loving His people today? Remember the song of Moses.

Finally he saw that his pleading apparently could not change God's decision. He did not question God's stand. Their sin was great. Moses knew that. They had attributed to the golden calf their deliverance from Egypt. The god of their enemies was the great power that rescued them from Egyptian slavery.

Moses had one thing left, and he did not hesitate to use it. He had his name in the book of life. As a last resort, he threw his own eternal life in the balances to save the people. God could not prevent him from doing it. Everyone has the right to choose life or death. The Lord cannot take that away from anyone. You will notice a dash in the middle of Exodus 32:32. It stands for a pause. Moses is sobbing out his heart; he knows how impossible it has been. God may accept his challenge and wipe him out. But he says, "God, please forgive, forgive I pray thee—or blot me out with the people." Rather than lose Moses, God forgave their sin and saved the people.

Because of his love for his people, Moses was willing to go down to destruction, an echo of Calvary. One man willing to give up his eternal life for others who were apparently his enemies. Some have been willing to give up *this* life for others, but Moses was willing to forfeit perpetual life. No wonder Scripture links his name with Christ's forever. "And they sing the song of Moses . . . and . . the Lamb."

Are you offended at the slightest affront, ready to shake the dust off your feet and leave God's people today? Does criticism of God's people, by enemies and offshoots, turn you against the church? Or, like Moses of old, can you say, "They are God's people, and I will stay by them until the heavenly Canaan appears."

But Moses had a great disappointment come to him. When the people crowded around him, threatening to stone him, he lost himself for a minute and smote the rock. "Ye rebels; must we fetch you water out of this rock?" He took the glory to himself. Immediately after he had uttered the words, he realized his great mistake. God said, "You have failed to sanctify Me in the people's presence. You shall not go into the Promised Land."

Our Lord holds leaders responsible for much more than He does the people. If you are anxious to be a leader, remember that God places greater accountability on you than on others. But Moses had his heart set on going into the Promised Land. It was the one thought that cheered him when Israel railed against him. Wait until they see that marvelous country flowing with milk and honey. Will it

The Song of Moses and the Lamb

not be glorious at last to hear them shout for joy?

But the consolation was denied him. It was more than he could bear. All looked forlorn and dark. But he still had hope. He decided to talk it over with God. Moses knew what prayer could do. So he began to plead with God: "God, let me go over and see the goodly land. Let me go over, God. O Father, let me go over. You know how hard pressed I have been with these people all these years, especially that fatal day. O Father, let me go over and see the goodly land."

Moses had such a hold on God's heart and he tugged so hard at His heartstrings that the Lord could not let him go on praying, or He might have given in. So He had to tell Moses to stop asking. When Moses learned that, he sobbed out, "But must I die in this land?" That same day the command came to Moses, "Get thee up . . . unto mount Nebo, . . . and behold the land of Canaan, which I give unto the children of Israel for a possession: and die in the mount whither thou goest up, and be gathered unto thy people" (Deuteronomy 32:49, 50).

"Moses had often left the camp, in obedience to the divine summons, to commune with God; but he was now to depart on a new and mysterious errand. He must go forth to resign his life into the hands of his Creator. Moses knew that he was to die alone; no earthly friend would be permitted to minister to him in his last hours. There was a mystery and awfulness about the scene before him, from which his heart shrank. The severest trial was his separation from the people of his care and love—the people with whom his interest and his life had so long been united. But he had learned to trust in God, and with unquestioning faith he committed himself and his people to His love and mercy.

"For the last time Moses stood in the assembly of his people. Again the Spirit of God rested upon him, and in the most sublime and touching language he pronounced a blessing upon each of the tribes, closing with a benediction upon them all."
"As the people gazed upon the aged man, so soon to be taken from them, they recalled, with a new and deeper appreciation, his parental tenderness, his wise counsels, and his untiring labors. How often, when their sins had invited the just judgments of God, the prayers of Moses had prevailed with Him to spare them! Their grief was heightened by remorse. They bitterly remembered that their own perversity had provoked Moses to the sin for which he must die."

"Moses turned from the congregation, and in silence and alone made his way up the mountainside. He went 'to the mountain of Nebo, to the top of Pisgah.' Upon that lonely height he stood, and gazed with undimmed eye upon the scene spread out before him. Far away to the west lay the blue waters of the Great Sea; in the north, Mount Hermon stood out against the sky; to the east was the tableland of Moab. . . . and away to the south stretched the desert of their long wanderings.

"In solitude Moses reviewed his life. . . . Not-

The Song of Moses and the Lamb

withstanding all that God had wrought for them, notwithstanding his own prayers and labors, only two of all the adults in the vast army that left Egypt had been found so faithful that they could enter the Promised Land. As Moses reviewed the result of his labors, his life of trial and sacrifice seemed to have been almost in vain. Yet he did not regret the burdens he had borne. He knew that his mission and work were of God's own appointing.... He felt that he had made a wise decision in choosing to suffer affliction with the people of God, rather than to enjoy the pleasures of sin for a season.

"As he looked back upon his experience as a leader of God's people, one wrong act marred the record. If that transgression could be blotted out, he felt that he would not shrink from death. He was assured that repentance, and faith in the promised Sacrifice, were all that God required, and again Moses confessed his sin and implored pardon in the name of Jesus.

"And now a panoramic view of the Land of Promise was presented to him. Every part of the country was spread out before him, not faint and uncertain in the dim distance, but standing out clear, distinct, and beautiful to his delighted vision. In this scene it was presented, not as it then appeared, but as it would become, with God's blessing upon it, in the possession of Israel. He seemed to be looking upon a second Eden. There were mountains clothed with cedars of Lebanon, hills gray with olives and fragrant with the odor of the vine, wide green plains bright with flowers and rich in fruitfulness, here the palm trees of the tropics, there waving fields of wheat and barley, sunny valleys musical with the ripple of brooks and the song of birds, goodly cities and fair gardens, lakes rich 'in the abundance of the seas,' grazing flocks upon the hillsides, and even amid the rocks the wild bee's horded treasures. . . .

"Moses saw the chosen people established in Canaan. He had a view of their history after the settlement of the Promised Land; the long, sad story of their apostasy. . . . He saw them, because of their sins, dispersed among the heathen, captives in strange lands. He saw them restored to the land of their fathers, and at last brought under the dominion of Rome. He was permitted to look down the stream of time and behold the first advent of our Saviour. He saw Jesus as a babe in Bethlehem. He heard the voices of the angelic host break forth in the glad song of praise to God and peace on earth. He beheld in the heavens the star guiding the Wise Men of the East to Jesus. . . .

"He beheld Christ's humble life in Nazareth, His ministry of love and sympathy and healing, his rejection by a proud, unbelieving nation. . . . He saw Jesus upon Olivet as with weeping He bade farewell to the city of His love. As Moses beheld the final rejection of that people . . . his heart was wrung with anguish, and bitter tears fell from his eyes, in sympathy with the sorrow of the Son of God.

"He followed the Saviour to Gethsemane, and beheld the agony in the garden, the betrayal, the mockery and scourging—the crucifixion. . . . Grief, indignation, and horror filled the heart of Moses as he viewed the hypocrisy and satanic hatred manifested by the Jewish nation against the Redeemer. . . . He heard Christ's agonizing cry, 'My God, My God, why hast thou forsaken Me?' He saw Him lying in Joseph's new tomb. The darkness of hopeless despair seemed to enshroud the world.

"But he looked again, and beheld Him coming forth a conqueror, and ascending to heaven escorted by adoring angels and leading a multitude of captives. He saw the shining gates open to receive Him, and the host of heaven with songs of triumph welcoming their Commander. And it was there revealed to him that he himself would be one who should attend the Saviour, and open to Him the everlasting gates. As he looked upon the scene, his countenance shone with a holy radiance. How small appeared the trials and sacrifices of his life when compared with those of the Son of God! . . . He rejoiced that he had been permitted, even in a small measure, to be partaker in the sufferings of Christ.

"[Then Moses witnessed the early Christian church, the Dark Ages, and the day to which you and I have come.] He saw the second coming of Christ in glory, the righteous dead raised to immortal life, and the living saints translated without seeing death, and together ascending with songs of gladness to the city of God.

"Still another scene opens to his view—the earth freed from the curse, lovelier than the fair

Land of Promise so lately spread out before him. There is no sin, and death cannot enter. There the nations of the saved find their eternal home. With joy unutterable Moses looks upon the scene—the fulfillment of a more glorious deliverance than his brightest hopes have ever pictured. Their earthly wanderings forever past, the Israel of God have at last entered the goodly land.

"Again the vision faded, and his eyes rested upon the land of Canaan as it spread out in the distance. Then, like a tired warrior, he lay down to rest. 'So Moses the servant of the Lord died there in the land of Moab, according to the word of the Lord. And He buried him in a valley in the land of Moab, over against Beth-peor: but no man knoweth of his sepulchre' " (Deuteronomy 34:5, 6).

"By Nebo's lonely mountain, on this side Jordan's wave
  In a vale in the land of Moab there lies a lonely grave;
  And no man knows that sepulcher, and no man saw it e'er;
  For the angels of God upturn'd the sod and laid the dead man there.

"That was the grandest funeral that ever pass'd on earth;
  But no man heard the trampling, or saw the train go forth:
  Noiselessly as the daylight comes when the night is down,
  And the crimson streak on ocean's cheek

grows into the great sun.

"Noiselessly as the springtime, her crown of verdure weaves,
And all the trees on all the hills open their thousand leaves;
So without sound of music, or voice of them that wept,
Silently down from the mountain's crown the great procession swept.

"Perchance the bald old eagle, on gray Bethpeor's height,
Out from his lonely eyrie look'd on the wondrous sight.
Perchance the lion stalking, still shuns that hallowed spot;
For beast and bird have seen and heard that which man knoweth not.

"But, when the warrior dieth, his comrades in the war,
With arms reversed and muffled drums, follow his funeral car;
They show the banners taken, they tell his battles won,
And after him lead his masterless steed, while peals the minute-gun.

"Amid the noblest of the land we lay the sage to rest,
And give the bard an honor'd place, with

costly marble drest,
In great minster transept where lights like glories fall,
And the sweet choir sings, and the organ rings along the emblazoned wall.

"This was the truest warrior that ever buckled sword;
This the most gifted poet that ever breathed a word;
And never earth's philosopher traced, with his golden pen,
On the deathless page, truths half so sage, as he wrote down for men.

"And had he not high honor? The hillside for a pall!
To lie in state, while angels wait, with stars for tapers tall,
And the dark rock-pines like tossing plumes over his bier to wave,
And God's own hand, in that lonely land, to lay him in the grave!—

"In that strange grave without a name, whence his uncoffin'd clay
Shall break again, O wondrous thought!— *before* the judgment day,
And stand, with glory wrapped around, on the hills he never trod.
And speak of the strife that won our life with the incarnate Son of God."

The Song of Moses and the Lamb

Moses died of a broken heart. His strength was still unimpaired, his sight perfect. But God, too, was brokenhearted when Moses died. He sent Jesus to bring Moses to heaven, loving him so dearly He could not wait, but said, "Jesus, raise him up and bring him to me that I may clasp him in My arms." Later, when circumstances looked discouraging to Christ, God sent Moses to speak words of comfort to His soul. The Exodus leader had been alone also in life. On the mountaintop he sat beside Jesus and repeated the story of his great disappointment and how his sacrifice for the people brought nothing but heartbreaks, with little appreciation. Christ took courage and went forward to save you and me. I love Moses for the great comfort he gave to my Jesus when Christ needed the help of a heart that understood. No wonder those two hearts that were broken will beat together in that blessed country. And we shall sing the song of Moses and the Lamb.

Will you be there to sing that song? All heaven will stop to listen as we unite our voices in the song that makes angels stand spellbound. What a thrill that will be when Christ raises His hand and the great chorus begins to sing in the land where song was born. On the sea of glass mingled with fire, as the glory of God shines into the calm crystal sea, will you join in that great chorus at last? Now is the time to learn that wonderful song of experience. Are you ready to sing the song of Moses and the Lamb? Love the unlovable, love the ungrateful, love the unappreciating, even those who seek to stone you? Through the great radio lanes of eternity, the smallest planets on the outer limits of the universe will stop and listen and wonder at a people who could love and forgive unto the end. That is singing the song of Moses and the Lamb.

> "O lonely grave in Moab's land! O dark Beth-peor's hill!
> Speak to these curious hearts of ours, and teach them to be still.
> God hath His mysteries of grace, ways that we cannot tell,
> He hides them deep, like the hidden sleep of him He loved so well."